SRI AUROBINDO
A Brief Biography

D1594137

SRI AUROBINDO
A Brief Biography

PETER HEEHS

DELHI
OXFORD UNIVERSITY PRESS
CALCUTTA CHENNAI MUMBAI

Oxford University Press, Great Clarendon Street, Oxford OX2 6DP

Oxford New York
Athens Auckland Bangkok Calcutta
Cape Town Chennai Dar es Salaam Delhi
Florence Hong Kong Istanbul Karachi
Kuala Lumpur Madrid Melbourne Mexico City
Mumbai Nairobi Paris Singapore
Taipei Tokyo Toronto

and associates in
Berlin Ibadan

© *Oxford University Press 1989*
First published 1989
Third impression 1997

ISBN 0 19 562307 X

Printed at Rekha Printers Pvt. Ltd., New Delhi 110020
and published by Manzar Khan, Oxford University Press
YMCA Library Building, Jai Singh Road, New Delhi 110001

Contents

Contents

Preface

Sri Aurobindo, known to some as a yogin and philosopher, to others as a political and revolutionary leader, was also a prolific poet and scholar. His many-sidedness has created difficulties for his biographers and for others who have written about his life. Those interested primarily in his spiritual experiences and teachings have played down his revolutionary activities. Those interested solely in his political thought and action have dismissed his life after 1910 in a few sentences. Those interested chiefly in his philosophy or poetry have given passing notice to his political career and spiritual development but gone on to treat him almost exclusively in intellectual terms. No one has tried to deal evenly with all the different aspects of his life: domestic, scholastic, literary, political, revolutionary, philosophical, spiritual.

I have attempted, so far as the scope of this volume has permitted, to give adequate attention to each of these aspects. My main problem has been to balance the conflicting claims of two different classes of readers: students of history and other social sciences, and spiritual aspirants. Readers in the first class require a work of scholarship: well researched, documented, and objective, making no unwarranted assumptions or unverifiable claims. A biographer who addresses this audience is expected to provide facts and interpretation based on facts. Readers in the second class are looking principally for spiritual guidance and uplift. They are interested mainly in anecdotes and examples, not facts and interpretation. They are apt to consider documentation unnecessary and to be offended by an objective tone. A biographer who wishes to reach them must share their assumptions and make appropriate claims.

I believe that the needs of both types of readers are legitimate and I feel that the present volume has something to say to each. My form, method and tone all are scholarly; at the same time, much of the book is devoted to Sri Aurobindo's spiritual life and thought. The scholarly approach, far from diminishing their importance, seems to me rather to bring out their distinctiveness.

A scholarly biography cannot be devotional in tone. But a biography of Sri Aurobindo that ignored his spiritual life could hardly be considered complete. For forty-five of his seventy-eight years he was engaged in the practice of yoga. The correct attitude of the scholar towards the inner experiences of this period is neither the passivity of the believer nor the aggressiveness of the debunker, but rather the critical openness of the seeker of truth. It is legitimate for a scholar to assume, as I have assumed, that spiritual experiences are (or, let us say, can be) genuine experiences of actual realities. I recognize that not all my readers will wish to make this assumption. I have therefore divided the book into two parts, the first of which requires no acceptance of, nor interest in, spiritual matters. This part, which covers the years 1872–1910, deals in chronological fashion with Sri Aurobindo's outer life, giving priority to his political career. The second part, covering the years 1908–50, is arranged topically as well as chronologically, and deals chiefly with his intellectual and spiritual development. In Part One I rely on traditional historical methodology; in Part Two I take the more flexible approach necessitated by my assumption of the possible validity of Sri Aurobindo's spiritual experiences. At the beginning of Chapter 9 I will speak of some of the problems I have encountered writing as a historian about a spiritual figure.

A biography that makes any claim to accuracy must be grounded on sober historical scholarship. But sobriety does not mean reductionism. The scholarly biographer of a saint or yogin, faced with evidence about outward happenings that is not in accord with his preconceptions, is not permitted to explain it away by invoking the *deus ex machina* of supernatural intervention. It seems equally dubious to me to explain away spiritual phenomena by invoking up-to-date *dei ex machina* of Marxist, Freudian or other provenance. When a sociologist interprets Sri Aurobindo's interest in spirituality as 'a way of handling a situation of cultural aggression',[1] he seems to me to be telling us more about his theoretical preconceptions than about Sri Aurobindo's discernible motives. It is even worse when a historian strays out of his field into the formula-ridden morass of pop psychology, suggesting that Sri Aurobindo's 'lifelong obsession with mother figures dates from his childhood', or that his rejection from the ICS was due to his 'fear of failure'.[2] If one is to deal successfully with inner experience—whether emotional, intellectual, or spiritual—one must deal with it in appropriately inner terms.

A non-devotional acceptance of the validity of spiritual experience permits the investigation of events and attitudes that orthodox scholarship cannot handle. The chief danger of this approach is the extension of methods appropriate to the study of inner experience to outward happenings. Most full-length biographies of Sri Aurobindo have been written from a spiritual point of view, and most do tend to 'read back the holy man into the earlier stages of his career'.[3] Allowed to go unchecked, this tendency would result not in biography but hagiography.

The charge of hagiography has often been levelled against Sri Aurobindo's previous biographers. 'Almost without exception', complains one critic, 'they have given readers the life of a saint, who they assume was an avatar. The human characteristics and personal drama have been lost in the process.'[4] I agree that the human side of Sri Aurobindo has not adequately been brought out in any existing biography; but this does not in itself convict the authors of the total lack of objectivity implied by the word 'hagiography'. In order to make the charge stick, it would have to be shown that a biographer was so intent on glorifying his subject that he distorted the entire picture.

Some two dozen biographies of Sri Aurobindo have been published in half a dozen languages. Only four of them have been based even partly on original research: A. B. Purani's *Life of Sri Aurobindo*, K. R. Srinivasa Iyengar's *Sri Aurobindo*, G. E. Monod-Herzen's *Shri Aurobindo* (French), and Girijashankar Raychaudhuri's *Sriarabinda o Banglay Svadeshi Yug* (Bengali).* Most of the rest are simply rewritings of Purani, with a few facts from Sri Aurobindo's autobiographical writings added here and there. Are the four original works hagiographic? Certainly not Raychaudhuri's. Though not so hostile to his subject as some have alleged, he certainly was not overly sympathetic. In the other three writers a bias in favour of Sri Aurobindo is clearly visible. This is not surprising since all of them were disciples or devoted admirers of their subject. But admiration, even discipleship, is not proof

---

* A few other early biographies, e.g. P. B. Kulkarni's Marathi work, *Yogi Aravind Ghosh* (1935), contain some original material.

of total lack of objectivity. It is true that none of the three biographers had anything unflattering to say about Sri Aurobindo, but neither did they engage in gratuitous glorification. The principal fault that could be alleged against them is lack of research and uncritical dealing with their limited resources. Only Purani made significant use of primary documents. None of the three sought out and analysed variant accounts. When their source erred they erred along with it. These shortcomings are more than balanced, however, by the advantage enjoyed by the three writers: they all had access to Sri Aurobindo and they were able to elicit from him a great deal of indispensable information. For this I and all future biographers must be indebted to them.

The present work is based on fifteen years' research in primary source materials. These are listed briefly in the bibliography. My reliance on these documents allows me to characterize this biography as scholarly. Otherwise it has few of the trappings of scholarship. It is a short work and does not pretend to be comprehensive. It is meant rather as a popular introduction to the subject. I hope it will mark the beginning of the critical study of a remarkable life.

A full list of the people to whom I am indebted would occupy a disproportionate amount of space. But I must acknowledge the help and encouragement I have received from various members of the Sri Aurobindo Ashram Archives and Research Library. Thanks also are due to the Trustees of Sri Aurobindo Ashram for permission to quote from Sri Aurobindo's works. Neither the Ashram nor its Archives is in any way responsible for ideas or opinions expressed or implied in these pages.

Part One

Part One

CHAPTER ONE

Indian Origins

Ever the synthetic thinker, Sri Aurobindo looked at the question of heredity from both sides. 'I may be the son of my father or mother in certain respects,' he once wrote, 'but most of me is as foreign to them as if I had been born in New York or Paraguay.' He concluded that 'heredity only affects the external being',[1] that is, the body, and certain tendencies of life and mind. The inner being had its own non-physical heritage. But though heredity was not the all-sufficient explanation of personality that some scientists would make it, it was nevertheless 'one of the physical conditions' of all natural development.[2]

Sri Aurobindo's immediate forebears included two men of uncommon ability. His maternal grandfather, Rajnarain Bose, was one of the most outstanding figures of nineteenth-century Bengal. His father, Dr K. D. Ghose, was known for his strong character and varied accomplishments. Both sides of the family also exhibited conspicuous flaws. Three of Rajnarain's children, Sri Aurobindo's mother among them, were mentally disturbed. Dr Ghose's disdain for conventional morality made him something of a misfit in the communities that he served. This blend of positive and negative traits should not surprise us. It did not surprise Sri Aurobindo. He knew that men of unusual energy often have vices as strong as their virtues and he evinced throughout his life an interest in the theory that genius is linked with madness. He wrote on one occasion: 'The fact that genius itself, the highest result of our developing consciousness, flowers so frequently on a diseased branch is a phenomenon full of troubling suggestions.' On another occasion he clarified: 'In order to establish genius in the human system, Nature is compelled to disturb and partially break the normality of that system, because she is introducing into it an element that is alien as it is superior to the type which it enriches.'[3]

A man's hereditary endowment is moulded by his environment. Sri Aurobindo was born in a place and time that fostered the development of remarkable individuals. Nineteenth-century Bengal was the scene of a social transformation whose effects were felt in every part of India. The fertile land of the Ganges delta, visited and coveted by several European powers during the sixteenth and seventeenth centuries, fell in 1757 to the armed merchants of the British East India Company. The first effects of this annexation were disastrous. Company administrators plundered Bengal of its wealth and used it as a base to extend their influence over the rest of the country. The culture of the province, eclipsed by that of its conquerors, fell into desuetude. But, as often happens when radically different civilizations meet and interact, this decline was followed by a period of renewal and vigorous growth.

The Bengal Renaissance, as this period is called, was the result of two complementary movements. The initial push was provided by the example and influence of Europe, exercised in particular through English education. This led, somewhat paradoxically, to a rediscovery by the people of the country of their own traditions. Sri Aurobindo's grandfather and father, like other thinking men of the times, were affected by both these trends; but they reacted to them in opposite ways. Rajnarain Bose, a product of the best European education then available in Calcutta, first repudiated Bengali culture, then became one of its most outspoken exponents. Kristo Dhone Ghose, after showing some interest in a neo-Hindu organization, journeyed to England and became a full-fledged anglophile. A closer examination of the lives of these two men, sufficiently interesting in themselves to merit more than passing notice, will give increased familiarity with the social milieu in which Sri Aurobindo was raised.

Rajnarain Bose was born in Boral, a village near Calcutta, in 1826. His father, Nanda Kishore Bose, worked as a clerk for the British East India Company. Attracted by the teachings of Rammohun Roy, Nanda Kishore became a member of the Brahmo Samaj, a Hindu reform sect founded by Rammohun, and for some time was the great man's secretary. Nanda Kishore's son Rajnarain received his education at the leading English-language school and college of Calcutta. A brilliant student, Rajnarain's reading extended far beyond the prescribed curriculum. Exposure to Western rationalism caused him to lose faith in Hinduism and he sought in Islam, Christianity, and European philosophy a new framework for his beliefs. Like many other members of his generation, he discarded the ethical as well as the intellectual standards of his native culture and took part in the excesses of that movement of student protest known as Young Bengal. The death of his wife and father during this period of mental and moral experimentation cast Rajnarain into anguished introspection. He found support in the Vedanta philosophy, and, after coming into contact with Devendranath Tagore, became a member of the revived Brahmo Samaj.

After working for three years in Calcutta, Rajnarain moved to Midnapore in south-western Bengal, where he became headmaster of the local English school. He remained in Midnapore for most of his active life, taking a prominent part in the town's civic activities. His sermons, delivered as leader of the local Brahmo congregation, were published and widely read. (Keshub Chunder Sen became a Brahmo after reading one of Rajnarain's pamphlets.) At this time missionaries such as Alexander Duff and Krishna Mohan Banerjea were carrying out a vigorous and sometimes vicious campaign against Hinduism and its Brahmo offshoot. Rajnarain, with his mastery of English and Sanskrit, was ideally suited to defend the Indian tradition against this Christian polemic. Seizing the offensive, he asserted that the Brahmo dharma, which embodied the essence of the original Hinduism of Vedanta, not only was superior to Christianity but was in fact the key to the 'science of religion'.[4] In matters of general culture also, Rajnarain championed traditional Bengali life over that of the dominant Briton. In 1866 he published a prospectus for a 'Society for the Promotion of National Feeling among the Educated Natives of Bengal', in which he advocated the use of the Bengali language (then fallen into disfavour among the educated élite), and the revival of indigenous medicine, music, gymnastics, etc. This prospectus was one of the first evidences of nationalist sentiment in India.

In March 1866, after the first schism in the Brahmo Samaj, Rajnarain retired from his headmastership, went to Calcutta, and became the chief spokesman for, and later the president of, the

Adi or original Brahmo Samaj. For twelve years he struggled to keep the Brahmos from breaking entirely with the Hindu community, going so far as to proclaim, in a famous lecture of 1872, that Hinduism itself was the highest form of religion. His speeches and writings helped launch the Hindu revival movement which heralded the end of educated Bengal's century-long infatuation with Western ways.

Closely associated with this movement was an upsurge of Bengali nationalism. An annual Jatiya Mela or National Gathering, patterned after ideas in Rajnarain's prospectus, became so popular that it was given permanent form in the Jatiya Sabha or National Society. This organization was a harbinger of the movements of the 1870s that culminated in the foundation of the Indian National Congress. Around this time a number of amateur 'secret societies' sprang up in Calcutta; one of them, of which the young Rabindranath Tagore was a member, was headed by Rajnarain. He thus was a trailblazer in both the political and the revolutionary movements that a quarter-century later would be led by his grandson Aurobindo.

In 1879 Rajnarain retired to Deoghar, a hill-station in Bihar, where he devoted his last years to the study of the Indian, Persian, and European mystical writings that he loved. Even before his death in 1899 he was looked on as a modern rishi, and had received the affectionate title by which he is still remembered: the Grandfather of Indian Nationalism.

In his posthumously published autobiography Rajnarain wrote that nothing in his life distressed him as much as the lapse of his beloved son-in-law Kristo Dhone Ghose from the Brahmo fold. Kristo Dhone was born in Patna in 1844. At the time of his marriage to Rajnarain's daughter Swarnalotta, he was deeply interested in the doctrines of the Brahmo Samaj; but during a two-year stay in Britain, where he earned the degree of M.D. from Aberdeen University, he conceived a disgust for everything Indian and adopted English habits of dress, speech, behaviour, and thought. Returning to India in 1871, he was appointed Civil Medical Officer of Rangpur in north-eastern Bengal (at present in Bangladesh). Here he proved himself to be an energetic physician and health officer. In his first year of service he wrote a report on the sanitary condition of Rangpur, a place which, at the time, was famous for its malaria. He recommended that the swamps around the town be drained and then saw to it that a drainage canal was cut. The infestation of mosquitoes was reduced and the incidence of malaria fell sharply. This and other successful projects gave him the reputation of being a man who got things done. The District Magistrate and other British officers held him in high esteem and, in 1876, made him a member of the town council. The next year Kristo Dhone became the first Bengali to be elected Vice-Chairman of the Rangpur Municipality. He and his wife were popular both with the British and the Bengali communities; as a link between the two, he became known as Rangpur's 'Suez Canal'.

Obedient to her husband's wishes, the beautiful young Swarnalotta learned how to behave like a proper memsahib. She spoke English, wore frocks, and even went riding. At the time of their arrival in Rangpur the couple had two sons, Benoybhushan and Manmohan. In 1872, with another child expected, Dr Ghose sent Swarnalotta to Calcutta to stay with his friend Mano Mohun Ghose, a prominent barrister who lived in the fashionable Chowringhee section of town. Here, on the morning of 15 August 1872, Swarnalotta gave birth to her third son. 'In a sudden inspiration' Dr Ghose decided to call the boy Aurobindo, a Sanskrit word for 'lotus'.[5] He also gave him an English-style middle name, Akroyd, after his friend Annette Akroyd, a lady who founded a Brahmo girl's school in Calcutta.

Shortly after Aurobindo's birth his mother returned with him to Rangpur. Here he passed his early childhood, about which little is known. During this period Swarnalotta showed the first signs of a mental disorder that gradually took complete possession of her. The exact causes of her insanity are not known, but the disease seems to have been at least partly hereditary since two of her siblings were similarly affected. Swarnalotta soon became incapable of taking proper care of her children. One of Aurobindo's earliest memories was of his mother beating his brother Manmohan with a candlestick. Aurobindo, declaring that he was thirsty, asked permission to leave the room. We do not know what effect his mother's madness had on Aurobindo; but a comment made by Manmohan years later shows that he at least was scarred by the lack of maternal affection: 'You may judge the horror of this, how I strove to snatch a fearful love, but only succeeded in hating and loathing, and at last becoming cold. Crying for bread I was given a stone.'[6]

Dr Ghose was of course distressed to watch his wife's condition deteriorate. At that time medical science could do little to help victims of serious mental illness. In 1883 the doctor's professional life also took an unhappy turn. A new British Magistrate came to Rangpur and was vexed to find that nothing could be done in the district without the assistance of Dr K. D. Ghose. At the Briton's instigation Dr Ghose was transferred to Bankura in north-western Bengal. Here he remained less than a year before being transferred again to Khulna in the south-eastern part of the province. This callous treatment at the hands of a race that prided itself on fair play confused and embittered Dr Ghose. He ceased to be an admirer of British culture; but by this time he was too far removed from his own to be able to rejoin it. He won the respect of the people of Khulna as a skilful doctor and dedicated member of local government, and won their love as a selfless philanthropist from whose door, it was said, no one ever went away empty-handed. But by now he was a profoundly unhappy man. Depressed by his wife's insanity, betrayed by his former friends, isolated from his neighbours, Dr Ghose found solace in drink. He died in 1892 at the age of forty-eight.

During the five years that Aurobindo lived with his parents at Rangpur, his mother was still partly in possession of her senses and his father still a contented government servant. Dr Ghose was at that time so convinced of the superiority of European culture that he refused to allow Bengali to be spoken in his house. Aurobindo grew up speaking English and a little Hindustani. Around 1877 his father had him and his brothers enrolled in the Loreto Convent School in Darjeeling. Benoybhushan, Manmohan, and Aurobindo must have been among the only Indian students, for the school catered mostly to the daughters and sons of English planters and officers. The classes were in English and must have included a good dose of Christian teachings. Aurobindo was of course still of kindergarten age and presumably spent more of his time playing than studying. In later years he recalled walks along the fern-hung pathways of Darjeeling, beautifully situated in the shadow of Kanchenjunga, amid what were then virgin hillsides of pine and deodar.

One of the doctor's chief reasons for sending his sons to convent school was to give them increased proficiency in English and familiarity with English ways. His ambition was for them to become great men ('beacons of the world',[7] as he put it) and in British India the greatest possible career was a position in the Covenanted Civil Service of India (ICS). Even 'natives' were eligible for this exclusive and high-paying service, but very few were able to pass the entrance examination—which was held in England and based on the English school curriculum. Dr Ghose's friend Mano Mohun Ghose had twice sat for the ICS test and twice failed it. He himself had been unsuccessful in his attempt to enter the Covenanted Indian Medical Service. He knew that if his boys were to make the grade they had to start their training early. This became the more necessary after 1876, when a change in the ICS regulations lowered the maximum age for contestants from twenty-one to nineteen. It would now be almost impossible for students who had completed their secondary education in India to compete with English public school boys who had specially crammed for the examination.

Dr Ghose realized that the only way to insure that at least one of his sons passed the examination was to have them educated from childhood in England. In 1879 he took them to Manchester and left them with a Congregational minister named William H. Drewett. He asked Drewett not to allow them to 'make the acquaintance of any Indian or undergo any Indian influence'.[8] Drewett agreed, and Aurobindo spent his formative years totally cut off from the culture of his birth.

CHAPTER TWO

Education in England

In 1879, after spending six years in rural Bengal, Aurobindo Akroyd Ghose found himself suddenly in the second largest city of Great Britain. Manchester, the centre of the Lancashire weaving industry, which had grown great at the expense of India, was more densely populated even than London. Its industrial districts were notorious for their ugliness, and even residential areas like Ardwick, where the Reverend Mr Drewett lived, were far from pretty. Drewett's house was at 84 Shakspeare Street, close to the church on Stockport Road of which he was the minister. The 'Octagonal Church', as it was called, was a Nonconformist chapel of the Congregational denomination. Based on the stern doctrines of Calvinism, the Congregational Church yet was noted for its openness to new ideas and for the importance it gave to education. Drewett himself was an accomplished Latin scholar and he taught that language, still the focus of education throughout Europe, to his young Indian charges. True to a promise he had made to Dr Ghose, Drewett gave them no religious indoctrination; inevitably, however, they absorbed much of the Christian atmosphere of the minister's household.

In 1881 Benoybhushan and Manmohan began studying at the Manchester Grammar School. Aurobindo, still only nine, was kept at home and tutored in Latin and history by Mr Drewett, and in French, geography, and arithmetic by Drewett's wife. He never was taught English as a separate subject but picked it up like a native in daily conversation. Before long he was spending much of his time reading. Almost from the start, he devoted himself to serious literature. As a ten-year-old he read the King James Bible and the works of the English poets. His first poem, 'Light', published in January 1883, shows both these influences. It is filled with Biblical imagery and written in the stanza of Shelley's lyric 'The Cloud'.[1] Another poem of Shelley's, 'The Revolt of Islam', helped turn Aurobindo's maturing thought in the direction of political action. Touched by something in Shelley's imaginative recreation of the French Revolution, Aurobindo decided to dedicate his life 'to a similar world-change and take part in it'.[2] He had by this time 'received strongly the impression that a period of general upheaval and great revolutionary changes was coming in the world', and he felt destined to play a part in these changes. This feeling was at first not specially connected with India, about which 'he knew nothing'; but soon his father—whose opinion of the British had changed radically as a result of his unjust transfer—began to send him newspaper reports of the mistreatment of Indians by Britons and to condemn the Indian government as 'heartless'. When Aurobindo learned of conditions in his homeland, his general commitment to revolutionary action was 'canalised into the idea of the liberation of his own country'.[3]

In 1884 Mr Drewett emigrated to Australia. On the way he stopped off in Calcutta and collected the money that Dr Ghose owed him for the upkeep of his children. For some time the doctor had been remiss about sending funds, at least in part because he gave away much of his salary to the needy of Khulna. When Drewett left England he arranged for the Ghose boys to be looked after by his mother. The three brothers were taken to London where, in September 1884, the two brighter ones, Manmohan and Aurobindo, were enrolled in St Paul's School.

Before entering St Paul's, Manmohan and Aurobindo were examined by the High Master, Frederick William Walker, who was looked on as one of the most outstanding English headmasters of his day. Impressed by Aurobindo's proficiency in Latin, Walker awarded him a Foundation Scholarship and placed him directly in the upper fifth form. Taking Aurobindo into his 'specials', the High Master taught him the rudiments of Greek and pushed him rapidly into the school's upper forms. Before long Aurobindo was studying the Latin and Greek classics, writing poetry and prose in both languages, and reading English literature, 'divinity' (Bible studies), and French. He did not study science; St Paul's gave little importance to this subject and was content to provide most of its scholars with a bare minimum of mathematical knowledge.

From the start Aurobindo did well at St Paul's: so well in fact that after the age of fifteen his school studies ceased to interest him. His teachers, who up till then had considered him 'a very promising scholar', began to lament that he was wasting his 'remarkable gifts' because of laziness.[4] Aurobindo now 'spent most of his spare time in general reading, especially English poetry, literature and fiction, French literature and the history of ancient, mediaeval and modern Europe'.[5] In English poetry his favourite authors were the Romantics: Keats, Shelley, Byron, *et al.* He also read a good amount of Elizabethan poetry and drama, and did not neglect modern and contemporary verse: Tennyson, Browning, Arnold, Swinburne, Morris, and Meredith. Well acquainted with English fiction and criticism, he preferred French writers in both types of prose. He also taught himself Italian, German and Spanish in order to read Dante, Goethe and Calderón in the original tongues. A boy with so ambitious a programme of study could not rightly be accused of laziness. And despite his lack of interest in class work, he did not slip academically. Although he never reached the top of his form, he did well in all his subjects and impressed everyone, masters and fellow-scholars alike, as brilliant.[6] He also wrote poetry and was active in the school's literary and debating societies.

In his reading of history Aurobindo concentrated on 'the revolutions and rebellions which led to national liberation', and made heroes of Joan of Arc, Mazzini, and others who fought against foreign domination. These historical studies fertilized the seed of his resolution to serve his homeland. By the time he turned fourteen it 'began to sprout', and before long he took a 'firm decision' to work for India's liberation.[7]

Religion did not appeal to Aurobindo. He was put off by the evangelism of Drewett's mother and, when he began to think for himself, he was repelled by the cruder doctrines of Christianity— for instance the notion that some souls are predestined to eternal damnation. As his studies progressed and he grew aware of 'the hideous story of persecution staining mediaeval Christianity and the narrowness and intolerance even of its later developments', he became so disgusted that he 'drew back from religion altogether'.[8] Before leaving school he began to think of himself as an agnostic. But his lack of faith in Christianity (he of course knew nothing about Hinduism) did not stand in the way of his moral development. Introspection made him aware of defects in his character—selfishness, fear, a tendency to tell lies—and he tried to eliminate them. Later he looked on his abandonment of selfishness at the age of thirteen as a turning point in his inner life; this came about not under the influence of religion but as part of his growing dedication to the great work in which he felt destined to play a role.

Aurobindo's preoccupation with intellectual and moral pursuits, his physical weakness, and his lack of interest in games might have caused the other boys to regard him as a prig had they not been won over by his innocence and candour. They did, however, consider him childish, and as a result tended to patronize him. The fact that he was younger than his classmates, together with his retiring disposition, caused him to keep pretty much to himself. The boys paid little attention to him, but, as time went by, they could not help noticing that he began to look 'more and more unhealthy and neglected'.[9] They did not realize that after 1887 Aurobindo and his brothers were living on the verge of poverty. Their father had virtually stopped sending them money. When they outgrew their old overcoats they could not buy new ones. At home there was no coal for the fire and hardly any food. During a whole year Aurobindo and Benoybhushan had to survive on 'a slice or two of sandwich bread and butter and a cup of tea in the morning and in the evening a penny saveloy [sausage]'.[10] The two brothers were at this time living as lodgers in a building owned by the Liberal Club in South Kensington. The club's secretary gave Benoybhushan a clerical job which earned him five shillings a week. This was hardly enough for two young men to live on. (Manmohan by this time had gone up to Oxford and was receiving most of the scanty resources that their father was sending.) For several years Benoybhushan and Aurobindo led quite Spartan lives and occasionally had to hide from their creditors.

Economic hardship did not prevent Aurobindo from successfully completing his studies at St Paul's. It had fallen to him to fulfil his father's ambition for one of his sons to enter the ICS. In 1888 Aurobindo joined the school's 'ICS class', composed of boys preparing for the entrance examination. Those who passed it would be obliged to spend two years at a university, studying subjects required by the Civil Service Commission. If Aurobindo was to do this he would have to obtain a full university scholarship. Late in 1889 he decided to try for one of the £80 Open Scholarships offered by King's College, Cambridge. He took the examination in December and came out on top of the list. Indeed, Oscar Browning, a noted scholar and writer, later told Aurobindo that his classical papers were the best he had seen in thirteen years as an examiner.

Assured of a place at King's, Aurobindo spent the first half of 1890 preparing for the ICS examination. It consisted of as many as seventeen papers occupying two full weeks of June. Aurobindo took ten of the seventeen and did well in most of them. Predictably, he was most successful in Greek and Latin, obtaining record marks in these two subjects. He scored high in English composition and French and picked up enough marks in English literature, English history, and Italian to offset his poor scores in mathematics and logic. Overall he stood eleventh of the forty-five selected candidates. (More than two hundred were rejected.) His future now seemed assured. After two years of probation at Cambridge he would fulfil his father's dream by returning to India a member of the 'heaven-born' bureaucracy.

King's College, founded in 1441, is among the older foundations of Cambridge University. As a classical scholar, Aurobindo was participating in an educational system whose traditions went back to the Renaissance. To master Greek and Latin, to read Homer and Sophocles, Virgil and Horace, to absorb the culture of classical Greece and Rome—these were considered the proper training of an English gentleman. And what one learned in the classroom and lecture hall was only part, and not the most important part, of the Cambridge experience. The university's atmosphere took hold of those who entered it and wrought a comprehensive change. A few years after leaving King's, Aurobindo reminisced:

[A boy] goes up from the restricted life of his home and school and finds himself in surroundings which with astonishing rapidity expand his intellect, strengthen his character, develop his social faculties, force out all his abilities and turn him in three years from a boy into a man. . . . He who entered the university a raw student, comes out of it a man and a gentleman.[11]

Aurobindo had only two years at his disposal, and this put special demands on him. As the recipient of a scholarship he had to prepare for the Classical tripos, taking that difficult honours examination after two instead of the usual three years. At the same time, as an ICS probationer, he had to follow a completely different curriculum and demonstrate his mastery of a half-dozen subjects in three periodical examinations. Fortunately he was by now so proficient in classics that he did not have to devote much time to his composition and translation assignments. Even without labour, he was able to win prizes for classical verse at the end of both his years at Cambridge. His ICS course cost him more effort since he had no background in the subjects he had to study: Law, Sanskrit, Bengali, Indian history and geography, and economics. He did well enough in all these subjects but his examination results, which grew worse as he went along, indicate that he was steadily losing interest in his ICS studies.

Before going up to Cambridge, Aurobindo had never questioned his father's decision that he join the Indian Civil Service. But when he saw the sort of men he would have to work with— 'unmannerly, uncultivated, unintelligent' mediocrities[12]—and realized how uncreative and dull the administrative grind would be, he began to regard his proposed career with some distaste. He also began to wonder whether a position in the ICS would permit him to fulfil his dream of working for his country's liberation. Not wishing to disappoint his father, he put away his doubts for the moment and went ahead with his studies. But at the same time he joined the Indian Majlis, a student society, at whose meetings he delivered patriotic speeches.

While at King's, Aurobindo gave much of his time to writing. He composed a number of lyric poems, a ballad, a verse play, and a philosophical dialogue entitled 'The Harmony of Virtue'. Clearly influenced by the dialogues of Plato, and of Oscar Wilde, 'The Harmony of Virtue' nevertheless gives evidence of the workings of an original mind. Aurobindo had little interest in philosophy per se; he considered most of it to be verbal acrobatics and empty system-building. In his opinion the real aim of philosophy was to assist men in their search for 'virtue', taken in its etymological sense of 'manliness' or character. This came, he wrote, through 'the perfect evolution by the human being of the inborn qualities and powers native to his humanity'.[13]

By not sending regular remittances, Dr Ghose, whether he intended it or not, helped his sons develop the 'virtue' that comes only from meeting and overcoming adversity. He was proud that Aurobindo was being 'borne' at Cambridge 'by his own ability',[14] but did not realize that his son's scholarship and ICS stipend were not sufficient to cover all of his and his brothers' needs. Aurobindo's advisor G. W. Prothero, Praelector of King's College, had several times written to Dr Ghose to send money, once in order to pay off 'some tradesmen who would otherwise have put his son into the County Court'. Writing about Auro- bindo's 'pecuniary difficulties' in a letter of 1892, Prothero asserted that 'he has had a very hard and anxious time of it for the last two years'. The Praelector was sure, however, that the young man's problems 'were not due to any extravagance on Ghose's part: his whole way of life, which was simple & penurious in the extreme, is against this'. Prothero, noting that through it all the young man's 'courage & perseverance have never failed' him, affirmed that the young scholar had 'not only ability but character'.[15]

After a year and a half of study at Cambridge, Aurobindo took the examination for the first part of the Classical tripos in May 1892. He secured a First Class (third division). According to one of his classmates he missed the top division only because he had to take the tripos at the end of the second instead of the third year. This circumstance also prevented him from receiving the degree of B.A., for at Cambridge 'the First Part gives the degree only if it is taken in the third year'.[16] Of course Aurobindo, as an ICS probationer, had no need of a degree. He had only to pass the final ICS examination and to go through such formalities as the physical and riding examinations, and he would be assured of a secure position in the highest-paying and most prestigious service in India.

After passing the tripos, Aurobindo was free to devote as much time as he wanted to his ICS subjects. He does not seem to have cared to study very much. In the examination, held in July, he did just well enough to get by. His final rank was thirty-seventh out of forty-four, a drop of twenty-six places from his entering rank. But this hardly mattered now. By the beginning of November all that stood between him and full membership in the Indian Civil Service was the examination in horseback riding.

The Civil Service Commission made it clear that 'no Candidate will be deemed qualified for the Civil Service of India who fails to satisfy the Civil Service Commissioners of his competence' with respect to riding.[17] All ICS officers passed part of their careers in remote districts that had to be toured on horseback. A high degree of riding ability was therefore essential. Aurobindo was by no means a good horseman. He had not had enough money to take a full course of lessons. His first attempt to pass the examination was a fiasco: he fell off the horse. Summoned for a second trial, he failed to present himself. After passing the written examination he went down to London, where he waited for instructions from the commissioners. Three times he was told to report for the riding examination. Three times he failed to do so. Finally the Senior Examiner of the Civil Service Commission called him and said that he would give him one last chance. 'This state of things could not be allowed to continue', he told the delinquent candidate.[18] The two made a firm appointment but Aurobindo failed to keep it. Instead, he went 'wandering in the streets of London' to pass the time. Late in the afternoon, knowing that it was too late, he went to the riding establishment and learned that the examiner had gone. Returning home he coolly informed Benoybhushan that he was 'chucked'. Benoy, 'with a philosophic attitude proposed playing cards', and the two of them sat down to a few hands.[19]

Why had Aurobindo lightly thrown away the chance to join the exalted ranks of the Indian Civil Service? He later explained that he simply 'didn't want to be in the British Government Service'.[20] His father, whom he deeply respected, would not have allowed him to reject the ICS himself, so he forced the commissioners to throw him out on the trivial grounds of failure in riding.

When James Cotton, Secretary of the South Kensington Liberal Club, learned that his young friend Aurobindo had been rejected from the ICS, he went to Whitehall and tried to get the commissioners to reconsider their decision. He also asked G. W. Prothero to write from Cambridge attesting to the young man's character and scholarship, and had Aurobindo petition Lord Kimberley, Secretary of State for India, for another chance to take the examination. All these efforts were in vain. Kimberley wrote that he was unwilling to overrule the commissioners' decision, adding that he doubted 'whether Mr Ghose wd be a desirable addition to the Service'.[21] He had no reason to think otherwise. By deliberately missing half a dozen appointments, Aurobindo had given the commissioners good reason to consider him irresponsible and inconsiderate. It must be added, however, that there were other factors behind Kimberley's decision. The rulers of India were by no means anxious to have 'natives' join the exclusive ICS. Kimberley himself wrote in 1893: 'It is indispensable that an adequate number of the members of the Civil Service shall always be Europeans'.[22]

Aurobindo learned of his final rejection early in December 1892. He was at that time living in London, having joined his brothers there in July. He had few commitments during the half-year he passed in the metropolis, and he spent much of his time reading. During his last days at Cambridge he had been introduced to Indian philosophy. In a required text on the 'six systems' (*shad darshana*), he had come across the idea of the Self (*atman*). Intrigued by this concept, he took up an English translation of the Upanishads and made what he later called 'a strong and very crude mental attempt to realise what this Self or Atman might be'. He was rewarded with what he later called a 'mental experience' in which he perceived that the Self alone was real.[23]

This experience, powerful as it was, did not diminish Aurobindo's conviction that he had a part to play in India's political revival. While in London, he came in contact with a number of Indian students, one of whom was Chittaranjan Das. Aurobindo did not share the enthusiasm that Das and others felt over the recent election of Dadabhai Naoroji to the British Parliament. Aurobindo did not think that British institutions could or would do much to satisfy India's political aspirations. He was convinced, even then, that India's destiny had to be worked out by Indians. When, however, the students got together to form a revolutionary society, Aurobindo became a member. The society, romantically called 'The Lotus and Dagger', was stillborn; but the fact that it was conceived at all was a sign of a new sort of thinking among India's educated élite.

As an opponent of British imperialism, Aurobindo was 'delighted' by his rejection from the ICS; but it placed him in an awkward position. Up till then he had never had to give any thought to his career. Now suddenly he was out of a job. Providentially, just at that moment the Maharaja of Baroda, Sayajirao

Gaekwar, was passing through London. James Cotton and Benoybhushan obtained an interview with the Gaekwar and solicited an appointment for Aurobindo. Impressed by the young man's educational background, the Gaekwar offered him a post for Rs 200 a month. Cotton and Benoybhushan, not realizing that Rs 200 was nothing for a man with Aurobindo's qualifications, accepted the offer. The Gaekwar later boasted that he had got an ICS man for a bargain.

Shortly after the meeting with the maharaja, Aurobindo and his brothers learned that their father had died. Dr Ghose, elated over the news that Aurobindo had passed his final examination, wrote him to return to India on a steamer scheduled to depart that autumn. When the time came, the doctor went to Bombay to bring his son home 'in triumph'.[24] Aurobindo did not arrive, however, and Dr Ghose went back to Khulna in a depressed state of mind. Later he was informed by telegram that the ship he was expecting his son to be travelling by had sunk. The information about the sinking was correct. The British steamer *Roumania* did in fact go down off Portugal at this time. Aurobindo, however, was not aboard. He had been obliged by the necessity of taking the riding examination to stay over in England. Unaware of this the doctor, heartbroken in the belief that his son had drowned, took to his bed and died.

Dr Ghose's death seems to have happened early in November 1892. Aurobindo probably would have learned of it a month later, just at the time that he was engaged by the Maharaja of Baroda. There was nothing for him to do now but return home. He booked passage on the steamship *Carthage*, which departed from London on 12 January 1893. On 6 February the ship reached Bombay. Two days later Aurobindo's service in Baroda began.

CHAPTER THREE

Career and Family Life

Aurobindo lived in Baroda for thirteen years, from February 1893 to February 1906. Beginning his service as a revenue-department trainee, he rose to be Vice-Principal of Baroda College. If he had been ambitious he could have risen still higher, but his career meant comparatively little to him. His interests at the time lay in literature, politics, and (towards the end of the period) philosophy and yoga. In all these fields his efforts in Baroda laid the groundwork for his later accomplishments. Writing much but publishing little, he developed the literary capacity that made possible his extraordinary output of 1906 to 1921. Working behind the scenes to establish a revolutionary movement, he helped prepare the way for the epochal events of 1906 to 1910 and after. His early efforts at spiritual practice became the basis of his *sadhana** of 1908 to 1950.

Aurobindo was never a social being, but during his stay at Baroda he took on many of the responsibilities of the family man and cultivated some noteworthy friendships. Most of these bonds were loosened when he took the plunge into politics, and all of them were severed when he devoted himself exclusively to yoga; but at Baroda these relations, together with his official duties, demarcated the structure of his life. In the present chapter we will examine this outward structure; in the next the inner and dynamic content of Aurobindo's years at Baroda.

Baroda was one of the largest of the 600-odd princely states that made up a third of the area and a quarter of the population of the Indian empire. During the first hundred years of the British raj,

---

* Practice of a discipline such as yoga.

rulers of these principalities had signed unequal treaties with the Company, gaining military security at the expense of political independence. Rather than annexing them outright, the British allowed such states to exist as protected vassals, in this way avoiding the trouble and expense of administering them. Ultimately protection became control. The British Crown, as 'paramount power', effectively governed the princely states through political agents or 'Residents'. The princes, safe on their make-believe thrones, were allowed to retain the pomp and panoply of kingship. They collected their subjects' revenue and, a few enlightened princes excepted, spent most of it on luxurious amusements. One of the exceptions was Sayajirao Gaekwar, the Maharaja of Baroda. His administrative system and educational programmes were in some respects in advance of those in British India. The Gaekwar owed much of his success to his ability to select talented officers. His bargain-priced ex-ICS man Aurobindo A. Ghose was one of the most notable of these.

Aurobindo began his work in the Survey Settlement Department, and later moved to the Revenue-stamps Department and the central Revenue Office. He found the work in all these places exceedingly dull. In 1895 he got his first chance to do something more suited to his abilities when the Gaekwar asked him to prepare a précis of a complex court case. The maharaja was so satisfied with the result that he gave Aurobindo a promotion and began summoning him whenever he needed help writing an important document in English. The ruler used to ask the young man for breakfast, sometimes sending the invitation by liveried horseman. After the meal was over Aurobindo stayed on for work. Although displeased by the young man's chronic lack of punctuality, the Gaekwar admired his ability and integrity and, as time went on, he gave him increasingly important assignments.

In 1897 Aurobindo was offered part-time work at Baroda's government college. He accepted with alacrity, glad of an opportunity to be free from administrative drudgery for an hour or two a day. The Gaekwar, however, was not willing to let him get away so easily, and it was not till the next year that Aurobindo was given an official appointment in the College. Between 1898 and 1901 he served as Professor of English and Lecturer in French. Despite his formal classroom manner, which discouraged intimacy, his students regarded him as an excellent teacher and looked up to him with respect bordering on adulation. Never an exciting speaker, he yet 'held the students spellbound' when he lectured on English poetry.[1] 'His exposition of the subject was so lucid and exhaustive,' wrote a former student, 'that no doubt was left about the meaning of any portion of the text and he inspired confidence in the minds of the students.'[2] Aurobindo found the lecturing less stimulating. Baroda College, a young affiliate of Bombay University, did not at the time attract superior students. Its curriculum, set by the university, followed British lines. Aurobindo, who had seen British education at its best at St Paul's School and King's College, was aghast to see how bad it could become when transplanted in Indian soil. Most of the students were concerned only with passing the university examinations. To this end they would obtain notes of the lectures delivered by the examiners in Bombay. One day, when Aurobindo was lecturing on Southey's *Life of Nelson* (a required text he did not especially admire), the boys informed him that his lecture was not in accord with the notes. He replied that he 'had not read the notes', but that 'in any case they were all rubbish'.[3]

Aurobindo appreciated the importance of passing examinations but he felt strongly that the essential thing for the students was to learn to think and express themselves clearly. The purpose of giving lectures was not to dollop out predigested information but to help the students develop their own points of view. The right procedure, he told one of them, was to 'listen to the lectures, take notes if you like and then make what you can of them'. He was unpleasantly surprised to see students 'take down everything verbatim and mug it up by heart. Such a thing,' he commented, 'would never have happened in England.'[4]

Aurobindo felt that the education given in Indian schools and colleges 'tended to dull and impoverish and tie up the naturally quick and brilliant and supple Indian intelligence, to teach it bad intellectual habits and spoil by narrow information and mechanical instruction its originality and productivity'.[5] In brief, it tended to crush rather than bring out the latent capacities of students. The real purpose of education was not to stuff the mind with knowledge but to provide 'the intelligence, character and general power' the student needed to find out the rest for himself.[6]

In class Professor Ghose rarely asked questions; but he was always ready to give assistance to students who approached him.

This, he thought, was the true role of the teacher: to be a helper and guide. He once enumerated the four objectives of a teacher. These may be paraphrased as follows:

1. He should not teach the student, but rather should help the student teach himself.
2. He should be concerned not with what the student remembers, but with what he understands.
3. He should find out if the student is interested in the subject, and, if not, create interest.
4. He should build the proper environment for learning.[7]

At Baroda, Aurobindo had hardly any chance to accomplish these objectives. Obliged by the rigid syllabus, and by the students' apathy, to spend most of his time explaining assigned texts almost word for word (he once commented ironically that he got his name as a teacher by explaining everything except prepositions and conjunctions), he still attempted, in his introductory and concluding lectures, to lead his students into the spirit of the works they were studying. He gave great importance to writing. 'Correct composition leads to correct thinking', he used to say. And he did not mollycoddle the students when he corrected their papers. Typical of his comments were: 'Fit for Standard III', and 'How have you come to the College?'[8] He advised the boys not to copy the style even of good writers but to think for themselves and get into the habit of putting their thoughts down on paper.

Aurobindo regretted that Indian universities, unlike their English exemplars, offered few opportunities outside the classroom for students to broaden their personalities. To help develop Baroda's collegiate environment he participated as much as he could in extracurricular activities such as the Union (debating society) and student newspaper. His speeches before the Union, while never masterpieces of oratory, held the audience's attention by virtue of their clarity and substance.

In April 1901 the Gaekwar, just returned from Europe, ordered Aurobindo to leave the college and join his personal staff. The young aide's first two assignments were to ghostwrite the maharaja's memoirs and to put together a report on the first twenty years of his administration. Aurobindo had no taste for this sort of writing and did not get far with either project. Asked later to compile Baroda's annual administrative report, he procrastinated so long that the British Residency had to send three reminders before receiving it. Aurobindo did, however, complete a long report on the Baroda economy which won him a commendation and promotion from the Gaekwar. He also drafted a number of speeches for the ruler to deliver at public occasions between 1901 and 1904. As a rule, such celebrity speeches were long, dull affairs, crammed with quotations from English authors and filled with glowing references to India's progress under the raj. The speeches that Aurobindo wrote had no such padding but dealt with the topic directly and frankly. One, delivered by the maharaja at the Industrial Exhibition at Ahmedabad in 1902, contained this forceful statement of India's fallen condition under the British:

Famine, increasing poverty, widespread disease, all these bring home to us the fact that there is some radical weakness in our system and that something must be done to remedy it. But there is another and a larger aspect of the matter and that is that this economic problem is our last ordeal as a people. It is our last chance. Fail there and what can the future bring us? We can only grow poorer and weaker, more dependent on foreign help; we must watch our industrial freedom fall into extinction and drag out a miserable existence as the hewers of wood and drawers of water to any foreign power which happens to be our master. Solve that problem and you have a great future before you, the future of a great people, worthy of your ancestors and of your old position among the nations.[9]

For a ruling native prince to speak so forthrightly in a public lecture at the beginning of the century was daring indeed. No wonder the Gaekwar sometimes asked Aurobindo to tone down the language of his drafts.

In 1903, during a summer tour of Kashmir, the maharaja gave Aurobindo a temporary appointment to the post of private secretary. In the retinue of an Indian native prince, the private secretary held one of the most important, and most desirable, positions. Working in close contact with the ruler, he could influence decisions on public as well as personal matters and generally had no difficultly advancing his own interests. More than one of the Gaekwar's private secretaries rose to be Dewan of the state. Aurobindo, indifferent to advancement, had little use for this bureaucratic plum. He resented the Gaekwar's constant demands on his time and there was 'much friction between them during the tour'.[10] As a result, the appointment was not made permanent, though Aurobindo's general responsibilities remained the same. As *huzur kamdar* or crown secretary he continued to draft edicts, memoranda, and letters for the maharaja. This work kept him busy until the beginning of 1905, when the ruler again departed for Europe.

At Aurobindo's request the Gaekwar reappointed him to the college in September 1904. In January of the next year Aurobindo began serving as Vice-Principal and Professor of English. A month later the principal went on leave, and Aurobindo acted in his place until February 1906, dividing his time between administrative tasks and teaching. In his lectures on literature he impressed a new batch of students with his method of 'going to the roots' of the text. The boys looked up to him 'almost with awe'.[11] One of them, Kanaialal Munshi, later a Congress leader, wrote: 'To the students of our College, Prof. Ghosh was a figure enveloped in mystery. He was reputed to be a poet, a master of many languages, and in touch with Russian nihilists.'[12] Some of the boys could sense the change in his manner that resulted from his practice of yoga. 'He had the eyes of a mystic', wrote one student, 'his mind seemed to be in a ferment.' Sitting in his tiny classroom like one abstracted, his left hand resting on the desk, his eyes fixed on a point across the room, Professor Ghose seemed to 'pour out his deepest thoughts' when he spoke on Burke's *Reflections on the Revolution in France*.[13]

When Aurobindo returned to India from England in 1893 he had virtually no family connections. His father had just died, his mother was 'dead to the world'.[14] Even his relations with his brothers were more formal than friendly. Growing up in England, they had not developed the strong attachments that are the rule in India. Aurobindo had a number of relatives in Bengal and Bihar but he was separated from them by hundreds of miles. In the circumstances it would not have been surprising if he had remained cut off from his kin. Instead, he made a special effort to get to know them. Family life remained always a thing of secondary importance to him; but he did get a taste of most of the domestic relations during his years at Baroda.

At the time of his return from England, Aurobindo's mother Swarnalotta was living near her father Rajnarain in Deoghar. When Aurobindo was taken to see her, the unfortunate woman, now totally insane, could hardly recognize him. His meetings with his grandfather, and with his sister Sarojini and brother Barin, came off much better. Aurobindo genuinely liked Rajnarain, and the old man was happy to see that his grandson was eager to learn Bengali and to become a thoroughgoing Indian. Sarojini was struck by Auro's shyness, and Barin found him 'a strange friend . . . at once a playmate and guide, with a quiet and absorbed look and almost always lost in deep study'.[15] Aurobindo's young cousin Basanti thought his devotion to reading a bit excessive. Watching 'Aurodada' unpack, she gaped in wonder when she saw that his trunks contained 'just a few ordinary clothes and then— books and more books!' She was happy to discover that Auro- bindo's studiousness did not prevent him from chatting with her and the other young people, or even from taking part in their games.[16]

At home in Baroda, free from such distractions, Aurobindo spent most of his free time reading and writing. His scholarly habits and retiring disposition prevented him from making many acquaintances; but the friendships he did form were notable for their strength and intimacy. Not long after his arrival in Baroda he met Madhavrao Jadav, a young officer in the Gaekwar's army. The two had a shared interest: both were convinced that India must be free. Madhavrao introduced Aurobindo to his brother Khaserao, in whose house Aurobindo lived during much of his stay at Baroda. In 1898 the barrister K. G. Deshpande, whom Aurobindo had known as a student at Cambridge, came to live and work in Baroda. The three Marathas and their Bengali friend formed a circle that was more than merely social. The Jadavs and Deshpande were connected with Bal Gangadhar Tilak and other political leaders of Maharashtra. Their friendship with Aurobindo established a link between the spirit of resistance that had never died out in the Bombay Presidency and the political enthusiasm that was beginning to animate Bengal.

Aurobindo's Maratha friends were all married. So were his two elder brothers. As a bachelor he must have been exposed to a lot of good-natured pressure to find a suitable wife. In 1900 he made up his mind to wed, and, after receiving numerous offers, selected Mrinalini, daughter of Bhupal Chandra Bose of Calcutta. Aurobindo and Mrinalini were married in April 1901. His age was twenty-eight, hers fourteen. After a month's honeymoon in Naini Tal, Mrinalini and Aurobindo's sister Sarojini came to live with him in Baroda. The two girls did not remain long. They found it difficult to stay in such unfamiliar surroundings, where no one could speak their native language. It was, moreover, a bad time to be in Gujarat. A countrywide famine had struck Baroda particularly hard and had been followed by a visitation of bubonic plague. Mrinalini and Sarojini were sent home and they did not rejoin Aurobindo for more than a year. This pattern—periods together followed by intervals of separation—continued throughout Aurobindo and Mrinalini's married life.

Despite the differences in their ages and interests, Aurobindo and Mrinalini had an affectionate relationship. But his absorption in literary and political work, and later in spiritual practice, gave him little opportunity to enjoy a conventional marriage. In a letter to his father-in-law he explained why he was unable to give family life as much value as other people do: 'I am afraid I shall never be good for much in the way of domestic virtues. I have tried, very ineffectively, to do some part of my duty as a son, a brother and a husband, but there is something too strong in me which forces me to subordinate everything else to it.' [17]

CHAPTER FOUR

A Poet and a Politician

Most people today think of Sri Aurobindo as a spiritual philosopher and yogin. Many remember him also as a leader in India's struggle for freedom, relatively few as a literary creator. But in fact these three aspects of his personality emerged in the opposite order. He was, as he once wrote, originally 'a poet and a politician, not a philosopher'.[1] And his philosophy grew out of his yoga, not the other way around.

Aurobindo's first published writings were a series of articles criticizing the Indian National Congress. In order to understand the thrust of his arguments, we will have to look briefly at the origins of Congress and at the state of Indian politics at the end of the nineteenth century. After the suppression of the Revolt of 1857, British India was ruled directly by the Crown. Men of the country were in theory entitled to hold government positions; but in practice all responsible posts were occupied by Britons. A legislative council, created in 1861, had a few ornamental Indian members; but it was a powerless advisory body with no influence on government policy.

The second half of the century was a time of great hardship in India. A series of famines took so many lives that the population of the country began to decline. Resentment against British rule built up, especially during the viceroyalty of Lord Lytton (1876–80). To many observers, among them an ex-ICS officer named A. O. Hume, it appeared that India was being pushed towards the brink of rebellion. Hume proposed establishing an association of 'highly educated Indians' that might serve as a 'safety-valve' to release pent-up forces of discontent. The idea of forming some sort of national organization had been in the air for some time. As we have seen, Rajnarain Bose had suggested something of the kind. So had K. D. Ghose's old friend Annette Akroyd, among a number of others. Hume's proposal therefore found a ready response; and in 1885 the first meeting of the Indian National Congress was held in Bombay.

During its first twenty years, Congress did little to promote the cause of Indian freedom. Delegates proclaimed their loyalty to Britain in language that today seems shockingly obsequious. Most of them genuinely believed that British rule was necessary for the country's stability and advancement. Such thinking was not without justification: the British after all had found India in a condition approaching anarchy and had brought about a number of beneficial changes. But in doing so they placed the people of the country in a position of enforced subordination.

The leaders of Congress, all of them members of the English-educated élite, had firm faith in the efficacy of 'constitutional agitation'; they believed, that is to say, that if they publicized their grievances through legal channels the justice-loving people of England would grant them redress. Aurobindo knew this was nonsense. In his first political article, published in *Indu Prakash* of Bombay in June 1893, only four months after his return to India, he wrote: 'If we are indeed to renovate our country, we must no longer hold out supplicating hands to the English Parliament, like an infant crying to its nurse for a toy, but must recognise the hard truth that every nation must beat out its own path to salvation with pain and difficulty, and not rely on the tutelage of another.'[2]

This article was followed by a nine-part series, published in the same paper between August 1893 and March 1894 under the title 'New Lamps for Old'. These articles contain the earliest reasoned critique in English of the aims and methods of Congress. Twenty-two-year-old Aurobindo did not mince his words:

I say, of the Congress, then, this,—that its aims are mistaken, that the spirit in which it proceeds towards their accomplishment is not a spirit of sincerity and whole-heartedness, and that the methods it has chosen are not the right methods, and the leaders in whom it trusts, not the right sort of men to be leaders;—in brief, that we are at present the blind led, if not by the blind, at any rate by the one-eyed.[3]

Aurobindo's direct criticism of the leaders of Congress, and of their British idols, was another new departure in his articles.

Congressmen like Pherozshah Mehta and Mano Mohun Ghose (the friend of K. D. Ghose in whose house Aurobindo was born) were, the young analyst declared, 'propagating . . . gross inaccuracies' when they proclaimed that history gave its support to the mendicant methods of Congress. Another prominent leader, Surendranath Banerjea, 'never evinced', Aurobindo wrote, 'any power of calm and serious thought'. He was even more unsparing of the British, calling Gladstone, the incumbent premier, 'quite unprincipled and in no way to be relied upon', and ridiculing the 'bare-faced hypocrisy' of educated India's 'enthusiasm for the Queen-Empress,—an old lady so called by way of courtesy, but about whom few Indians can really know or care anything'.[4] This was written at a time when Congressmen like Banerjea referred to the Queen as 'Our Sovereign', 'Our Mother', and 'Victoria the Good'.

Finally, however, the British were 'really not worth being angry with', because, Aurobindo declared, 'our actual enemy is not any force exterior to ourselves, but our own crying weaknesses, our cowardice, our selfishness, our hypocrisy, our purblind sentimentalism'.[5] This was perhaps the first articulation in India of what later became known as the policy of self-help. The people of the country had no one but themselves to blame for their condition, and no one but themselves to look to if they wanted change. The first step towards achieving self-sufficiency was to make Congress an effective political instrument. This meant, primarily, making it a popular body. The élite would have to lift up the lower classes; for it was only a broad-based movement, not the palaver of a smug minority, that could bring about the country's liberation. This call for the engagement of the masses was the third new departure in Aurobindo's articles, one that proved prophetic of the successful course of action adopted by Congress after 1919.

In 1893, however, very few were willing to consider such radical proposals. 'New Lamps' created a temporary sensation; but it troubled the powers that be. M. G. Ranade, the Maratha judge and reformer who was probably the most influential Indian in Bombay, warned the owner of *Indu Prakash* that he might be prosecuted for sedition if he continued to publish Aurobindo's articles. The owner, not surprisingly, told the editor, K. G. Deshpande (Aurobindo's friend from Cambridge, who had not yet moved to Baroda), that the series would have to be stopped.

Deshpande was able to get a reprieve only by persuading Aurobindo to modify his approach. Aurobindo wrote a few more,
somewhat academic articles, but he soon 'lost interest in these
muzzled productions... and finally dropped the whole affair'.[6]

Convinced by the reception of 'New Lamps' that India was not
ready for forthright political thought or action, Aurobindo
resolved to work from behind the scenes, contacting leaders like
Tilak and organizing cadres of workers in Baroda and Bengal. In
1902 he joined a secret society that had existed in western India
since the time of the Great Revolt. The leader of this group,
known by his title Thakur Sahib (he was a noble in a small Rajput
native state) shared Aurobindo's conviction that the direct road to
freedom was armed revolution. Around this time Aurobindo
made a trip to Rajputana to examine the possibility of an uprising
in the Indian army. He seems to have hoped that the Gaekwar of
Baroda would give financial and other support to such a venture.
The maharaja was too cagey to commit himself, but he did look
the other way when Aurobindo and his friends arranged for a
Bengali named Jotindranath Banerji to be admitted to the Baroda
army. In 1901, after receiving military training, Banerji returned
to Bengal as Aurobindo's first emissary in the work of revolutionary organization. For several years the results were disappointing.
Aurobindo sent his brother Barindrakumar to help Banerji in
1903; but the two did not get on and Aurobindo had to go to
Bengal himself in order to iron things out. From this time he began
to spend his vacations touring the districts of his home province,
meeting people and recruiting prospective workers. What he saw
was not at all encouraging. 'It was a hell of black death all around',
he recalled later. 'The prevailing mood was apathy and despair.'[7]
At times he momentarily lost heart himself. In an open letter
written at this time, but not published, he gave voice, in a tone of
bitter irony, to the indolence and selfishness of middle-class India:

Let us leave these things and look to our daily bread; this nation must perish
but let us at least and our children try to live while live we can. . . . We are
disunited beyond hope of union and without union we must ere long perish.
It may be five decades or it may be ten, but very soon this great and ancient
nation will have perished from the face of the earth. . . . Meanwhile it is well
that the Congress should meet once a year and deceive the country with an
appearance of life; . . . for so shall the nation die peacefully of a sort of
euthanasia lapped in lies and comforted with delusion.[8]

During all these years Aurobindo took no active interest in Congress. He did go to the Ahmedabad session in 1902, apparently because the Gaekwar was the opening speaker at the Industrial Conference that preceded the Congress. Ironically, the maharaja's address (which was written by Aurobindo)* had more political substance than any of the official Congress speeches. The Gaekwar said plainly that India's ills were partly 'the result of the acquisition of political power by the East India Company and the absorption of India into the growing British Empire'. A few days later Surendranath Banerjea, in his Congress presidential address, proclaimed: 'We plead for the permanence of British rule in India.' Aurobindo met Tilak at this Congress. The Maratha leader took him out of the pavilion and spoke to him at length about the work he was doing in Maharashtra.[9]

Aurobindo published nothing on politics in the decade that followed the suppression of 'New Lamps for Old', but he was continuously engaged in one form of writing or another. In July 1894 he brought out the first of a series of seven articles on the Bengali novelist Bankim Chandra Chatterjee, who had died in April of that year. Aurobindo had read one or two of Bankim's works and, despite his still imperfect mastery of Bengali, he was able to appreciate the magnitude of Bankim's achievement. Not only did he create the Bengali, and so the Indian, novel; he also, along with the poet Madhusudan Dutt, re-created the Bengali language. This was a matter of more than literary interest. Bankim and Madhusudan, wrote Aurobindo, had set in motion a 'revolution of sentiment which promises to make the Bengalis a nation'. And since Bengal was the intellectual and artistic bellwether of India, the consequences of this revolution would be felt in every corner of the country.[10]

Aurobindo's articles on Bankim show a grasp of the culture of nineteenth-century Bengal that was remarkable for one who had visited the province only once. They also reveal some blind spots in his appreciation, particularly in regard to Indian art. 'The Hindu imagination', he wrote, 'has had no gift' in the visual arts[11]—an opinion he repudiated after his artistic eye was opened to the genius of Indian painting and sculpture.

* See the previous chapter.

Aurobindo's attraction to the literature and culture of his home province drove him to perfect his knowledge of Bengali. He read books and journals, engaged a tutor to help him with the spoken language, and even tried his hand at writing Bengali verse. He knew, however, that he could never do anything great in a learned language and he put most of his literary energy into writing English. In 1898 he published his first book of poetry, *Songs to Myrtilla*. Most of the poems in this collection had been written in England and showed the author's indebtedness to Western literature; but there were also a few pieces written in India on Indian themes. Aurobindo's reading of Bengali literature was beginning to bear fruit. Three of the poems in *Songs to Myrtilla* eulogized Bankim and Madhusudan, and two were 'imitations' of lyrics by Chandidasa. He also translated at this time a number of devotional songs by mediaeval lyricists such as Vidyapati and Jnanadas.

Around 1900 Aurobindo shifted the focus of his studies from Bengali to Sanskrit. As one nurtured on Homer and Virgil, it was natural for him to be drawn first to the Indian epics. The poet in him responded to his reading of the Ramayana and Mahabharata by translating passages from both into English verse. The scholar in him became interested in the question of the Mahabharata's authorship, a literary problem that had nationalistic overtones. Vyasa's epic, he wrote, was, India's 'most considerable and important body of poetry', and, as such, 'the pivot on which the history of Sanskrit literature and incidentally the history of Aryan civilisation in India, must perforce turn'.[12] It was therefore a matter of concern to him that many Indian scholars accepted without question the claims of European Sanskritists that most of the Mahabharata consisted of interpolations that had little poetic value. Aurobindo resented this cultural imperialism, writing, 'It is not from European scholars that we must expect a solution of the Mahabharata problem.'[13] It could only be discovered by a man steeped in the traditions of the country who patiently went through the entire epic, sifting out the passages that bore Vyasa's hallmark. Aurobindo outlined a method for doing this in an essay and began the work of appraisal; but he was soon distracted from this rather tedious labour by other projects more suited to his poetical bent.

A year or two after he took up the study of the Hindu epics, Aurobindo began to immerse himself in the literature of the classical period, reading the poems and dramas of Kalidasa, the epigrams of Bhartrihari, and the works of Magha, Bhavabhuti and others. Around 1901 he completed a translation of Bhartrihari's *Nitishataka*; but it was to Kalidasa, the pre-eminent poet of this golden age of Sanskrit, that he returned again and again. He translated the *Meghaduta* and *Vikramorvasi* into English verse, and wrote half a dozen chapters for a projected work of criticism meant to bring India's greatest secular poet to the notice of the English-speaking world. But before he could complete this ambitious undertaking, his ever-active mind was drawn by yet another type of Sanskrit literature—the sacred writings of Vedanta.

It will be recalled that Aurobindo was exposed to the ideas of Vedanta while still in England. At that time he passively accepted the notion that the Self or *atman* alone was real, the world an illusion, and the purpose of spiritual practice to obtain liberation or *mukti*. Such an aim was unacceptable to one who had resolved to work for his country's freedom. But while reading the *Gita* at Baroda he saw that most interpretations of this essentially Vedantic scripture missed the distinctive nature of its teaching. They 'have laid stress on the goal', wrote Aurobindo, 'but they have not echoed Sri Krishna's emphasis on the necessity of action as the one sure road to the goal'. This mistake had to be set right. If the traditional wisdom of India was to last, 'and we are not to plunge into the vortex of scientific atheism and the breakdown of moral ideals which is engulfing Europe, it must survive as the religion of Vyasa for which Vedanta, Sankhya and Yoga combined to lay the foundations, which Sri Krishna announced and which Vyasa formulated.'[14]

Aurobindo, who throughout his life had shown scant interest in religion, had become an advocate of Hinduism. This return to the religion of his forefathers was connected, as shown by the last quotation, with his rejection of Western cultural values. Basing itself on materialistic science, Europe was apparently on the way to a complete domination of the world and its peoples. Ruthlessly exploiting Earth's resources, harnessing the power of steam and electricity, it had achieved a mastery over nature unknown to previous civilizations. Science had freed Europe from the shackles of institutional Christianity but had not provided a new system of values to replace the one it had rendered obsolete. The result, wrote Aurobindo in a passage that has a strikingly contemporary ring, was an upsurge of 'morbid animalism' demonstrating

Europe's 'neurotic tendency to abandon itself to its own desires'.[15]

It seemed to Aurobindo that Hinduism alone among the 'great embodiments of the old religious & moral spirit' did 'not on the side of reason stand naked to the assaults of Science'. Hinduism therefore could serve as the framework of a new world outlook. But by Hinduism Aurobindo did not mean 'the ignorant & customary Hinduism of today', but rather 'the purer form of Vedanta, which is now [c. 1902] under the pressure of Science reasserting its empire over the Hindu mind'.[16]

Aurobindo considered Vedanta to be the essence of Hinduism. It comprised, he wrote, 'the fount of our philosophies, the bedrock of our religions, the kernel of our thought, the explanation of our ethics and society, the summary of our civilisation, the rivet of our nationality'.[17] It thus subsumed his principal interests: politics, literature, and philosophy. From around 1903 Aurobindo turned with increasing frequency to the chief sources of Vedanta, the Upanishads. He had no difficulty reading them or translating some of 'the simpler and more exoteric' texts into English. The real problem lay in discovering the original significance of their sometimes symbolic, often obscure, but always pregnant language.

Two obstacles stood in the way. First, Western scholars like Max Müller had convinced many even in India that much in the Upanishads was 'unmeaning, artificial and silly'. Without actually saying it, Müller implied that only those passages that could readily be grasped by the Western mind could be considered valid. Aurobindo had no trouble dismissing this blinkered cultural chauvinism. Harder to deal with were the claims of the various orthodox schools in India that the Upanishads could be reduced to one or another set of dicta, each permitting only one interpretation. The most authoritative of these schools, the Adwaita philosophy of Shankaracharya, stressed the illusory nature of the universe and the futility of action. Like most students, Aurobindo began by accepting Shankara's point of view. But as his study progressed he saw that the commentator, intent on establishing his own philosophy, had often departed from the plain sense of the texts. Aurobindo did not reject cavalierly an interpretation that had commanded respect for more than a millennium; but he did say that a student in search of the truth must 'refuse to follow even Shankara, when his interpretation involves so many violences to the language of Sruti [scripture, i.e. the Upanishads] and so wide a departure from the recognised meaning of words'.[18]

It has always been acknowledged that Indian philosophy is not merely an intellectual matter but is based on spiritual experiences that can be achieved, eventually, by those who make the necessary effort. Experience leads to the realization of the truths that philosophy systematizes. The goal of spiritual practice is the experience of union with the eternal Reality or brahman. This goal, and the various practices by which it can be attained, are known as yoga.

As interested as Aurobindo was in getting at the truth behind Vedanta, he was at first not willing to take up yoga since he assumed, accepting still the Adwaita interpretation, that it would oblige him to renounce life and action. Even when a number of spiritual experiences came to him spontaneously between 1893 and 1903, 'such as a feeling of the Infinite pervading material space and the Immanent inhabiting material objects and bodies',[19] he did not immediately embrace a life of spiritual seeking. But around 1904 he realized that he might be able to use the spiritual power that was said to be one of the results of yoga to help carry out his political programme. As he wryly observed years later, his was 'a side-door entry into the spiritual life'.[20] He began with daily practice of the breathing exercises known as *pranayama*. The results were striking: great fluency in writing, improved health, and a general feeling of lightness. But except for a minor opening of the inner vision, he obtained no spiritual experiences from pranayama. Nevertheless, he continued to practice it, at one time for as much as six hours a day.

At the time that Aurobindo took up yoga, India's national politics had reached a nadir of impotence. Things might have continued in the same groove for years, even for decades, if the government had not made a fatal blunder. The partition of Bengal was originally intended as a straightforward administrative measure. But Lord Curzon, the Viceroy, chose to use it as a means to pay off old scores against the politically conscious Hindus of Bengal. The agitation that resulted, at first confined to one class of Bengalis, ultimately spread to all classes and every province, with unprecedented results. As the then little-known barrister Mohandas Gandhi put it, the day Bengal was partitioned 'may be considered to be the day of the partition of the British Empire'.

When the government's proposal was made public, Aurobindo saw that the issue of partition could be used to quicken the pulse of India's political life. He instructed his representatives in Bengal to step up their recruitment drive and wrote a pamphlet, 'No Compromise', that was printed and distributed in Calcutta. Between mid 1904 and mid 1905 it looked like the government might reconsider its decision and the anti-partition agitation levelled off. During this lull Aurobindo's brother Barindrakumar got the idea of establishing an order of *sannyasis* who would dedicate themselves to national work. He persuaded Aurobindo to write a statement of the ideals of this order. The resulting pamphlet, 'Bhawani Mandir', was later cited by the writer of a secret police report as containing 'the germ of the Hindu revolutionary movement in Bengal'.[21]

British observers regarded any combination of religion and politics as a deliberate 'perversion of religious ideals to political purposes'.[22] Some modern Indian historians have revived this line of thinking. But religion in India, unlike religion in England, or religion as viewed by European social scientists, is not something separate from the rest of life but rather its focus. When European-educated Indians rediscovered their religious roots it was inevitable that they would infuse the national movement with religious sentiment. Aurobindo's own interests in nationalism and yoga were rapidly converging. He met at this time a *naga sannyasi*, from whom he received a mantra meant to help in the revolutionary cause. He also met, at Chandod on the banks of the Narmada, a yogin named Brahmananda who impressed him greatly. Aurobindo and Deshpande decided to open a school in Chandod where students could learn about India and its culture while receiving instruction from one of Brahmananda's disciples.

In August 1905 the British government announced that Bengal would be partitioned as planned. Protests rocked the entire province. Aurobindo saw that the time had come for him to leave Baroda and he accepted an offer to become first principal of the newly founded Bengal National College. Honouring his commitments in Baroda, he remained on duty until the principal returned from his furlough. During the first months of 1906, while waiting for his own leave to be sanctioned, he continued his teaching, practised yoga, and wrote, in an incredibly short time, a five-act play, *Rodogune*. In March he left Baroda, went to Calcutta, and plunged into the fray.

CHAPTER FIVE

Bande Mataram

The Indian national movement had two sides: an open political
agitation and a secret revolutionary activity. Aurobindo was a
pioneer in both but at the start of his career, and for many years
afterwards, he gave priority to revolutionary methods. This prefer-
ence was not something he could speak of publicly; but even in
'New Lamps for Old' he made his attitude clear enough by writing
that just 'five short years' of violent revolution in France had done
more 'to change entirely the political and social exterior' of that
country than seven centuries of parliamentarianism in England.[1]
He believed that a subject nation had the right to win freedom by
violent means and he thought that a general insurrection, aided by
a military revolt, had a good chance of success in India.* Accordingly, between 1894 and 1905 he stood aloof from Congress
politics and devoted whatever time he could spare from his work
and studies to revolutionary organization.

The spirited public response to the anti-partition agitation of
1905 made political work attractive for the first time, and between
then and 1910 Aurobindo acted primarily as a political journalist
and as one of the leaders of the advanced nationalist party known
to history as the Extremists. In the present chapter we will sketch
the first phase of these open political activities, starting with his
arrival in Calcutta in 1906 and ending with his arrest in 1908. In the
next chapter we will look briefly at the revolutionary activities that
were being carried out concurrently under his direction.

Aurobindo continued his practice of yoga throughout these

---

* He conceived this idea, he explained in the 1940s, at a time when 'the military
organization of the great empires and their means of military action were not so
overwhelming and apparently irresistible as they now are' (*On Himself* 21).

hectic years and, in January 1908, at the height of his political influence, he had his first fundamental spiritual experience. We will postpone consideration of his sadhana until Chapter 9; but it should be borne in mind that even while outwardly engrossed in action he was inwardly concentrated on yoga.

When Aurobindo arrived in Calcutta in March 1906 the Swadeshi Movement had been in progress for seven months. Thousands had vowed to purchase only indigenous (*swadeshi*) goods and to boycott British manufactures. The idea of swadeshi was not new; the promotion of indigenous products had begun in the 1880s or even earlier. But before August 1905 it had never captured the mind of the public nor been used, in the form of boycott, as a political weapon. The immediate cause of the agitation was the partition of Bengal and to most Congress leaders swadeshi was legitimate only in this context. Only a few advanced politicians saw it as having a wider application. One of these was Aurobindo. He was present at the 1905 session of Congress at Benares, where a resolution supporting boycott was passed. This helped to convince him that energetic leadership might turn Congress into an effective political force.

The British government responded to the movement with repression, especially in the new province of Eastern Bengal and Assam. Gurkha police were quartered in the district where the boycott had been especially successful, ostensibly to protect purchasers of foreign goods but actually as a punitive measure. The government exacerbated growing tensions between Hindus and Muslims by openly favouring the latter. At the same time it systematically browbeat swadeshi leaders and issued numerous ordinances, some of doubtful legality. It was made an offence to shout 'Bande Mataram' (Hail Mother!), the refrain of a song by Bankim Chandra Chatterjee that had become the slogan of the movement. The authorities of both Bengals issued circulars prohibiting students from taking part in demonstrations. Boys who defied the circulars were expelled. This was one of the principal reasons for the creation of the Bengal National College. On 11 March 1906, just days after his arrival in Calcutta, Aurobindo attended the meeting at which the National Council of Education, the governing body of the College, was effectively founded. In the months that followed, while work on the College went forward, he attended many meetings of the Council's Executive Committee, presiding over several of them.

In April Aurobindo left Calcutta to take part in the Bengal Provincial Conference at Barisal. All the big Calcutta leaders went with their supporters: the moderate Surendranath Bancrjea, his middle-of-the-road rival Motilal Ghose, and the radical Bipin Chandra Pal. Aurobindo, still relatively unknown, and present at Barisal mainly as an observer, was associated with the Pal faction. On 14 April all the delegates marched to the pavilion, crying 'Bande Mataram' in defiance of the government's order. The police allowed the leaders to pass and then attacked the rank-and-file with iron-shod *lathis*. Many men were injured, some seriously. 'This outrage', wrote an observer, 'inflamed even the leaders of the "Moderate" party, one of whom, Bhupendranath Basu, declared: "This is the end, the beginning of the end of the British Rule in India". The feeling all over India was electric. . . . I recall that while all the others were excited, Sri Aurobindo was unperturbed; . . . he was satisfied with the evolution of thought and activity precipitated at Barisal.'[2]

After the conference, Bipin Chandra Pal, Aurobindo, and some others toured the districts of eastern Bengal. Pal, a powerful orator, addressed large and enthusiastic crowds wherever they went. In one district the magistrate issued an order prohibiting meetings. Pal thought it prudent to move on to the next locality but Aurobindo insisted that the meeting be held as planned, and Pal acquiesced. Unable to deliver speeches in Bengali, Aurobindo remained in the background during the tour, 'a silent distant figure lost in his own thoughts, speaking the fewest of words'.[3]

Aurobindo returned to Calcutta at the end of May and resumed his work with the National Council of Education. It soon became evident that the moderate-dominated Council, afraid of giving undue offense to the British, was willing to make only tinkering changes in the syllabus in the name of 'national education'. Thus hamstrung, the National College was opened on 15 August 1906, the thirty-fourth birthday of its first principal. Besides discharging his administrative duties, Aurobindo taught English, French, and history. He regretted the Council's timidity but did not think it profitable to oppose it. Nor did he have the time to do so; for the same month that he began work at the College he became involved in another, much more dynamic, vehicle of nationalism.

The advanced group in Bengal needed a daily English newspaper to compete with Banerjea's *Bengalee* and Ghose's *Amrita Bazar Patrika*. A Bengali journal, *Jugantar*, had been founded in March at Aurobindo's suggestion, but the purpose of this paper was to disseminate revolutionary ideas, not to formulate party policy. An English daily was needed to reach the educated classes both inside and outside Bengal, and in July Bipin Pal and his supporters decided to start one. The name chosen for the new journal was *Bande Mataram*, symbol both of devotion to the motherland and of defiance of the British authorities. Early in August, Pal asked Aurobindo to contribute a leader to *Bande Mataram* every day. Aurobindo consented.

Bande Mataram was an immediate success; but owing to bad management it was soon in financial difficulties. Aurobindo urged his collaborators to form a joint-stock company to assure the paper of adequate resources. At the same time he persuaded them to make it their party organ. Hitherto the advanced group in Bengal had been disorganized and nameless. Aurobindo insisted that they form themselves publicly into a party, join hands with their counterparts in Maharashtra, and proclaim Tilak as their leader. The party should place a stimulating programme before the country and adopt a new strategy *vis-à-vis* the moderate leaders. Instead of clashing with them periodically at Congress sessions, it should openly challenge their supremacy and wrest control of the organization from them. All of Aurobindo's suggestions were carried out. The 'New Party' took form in the autumn of 1906. Its rapid growth and dynamism so unnerved the moderate leaders that they began to stigmatize its members as 'extremists', a label that has adhered to them ever since. *Bande Mataram* became recognized as the voice of Extremism not only in Bengal but also in other parts of the country. Aurobindo set forth the ideals of the party in fiery but well-reasoned language that even the moderates, indeed even the British, were forced to admire. In October or November he became *de facto* editor of the paper after a power struggle in the party (which took place while he was too ill to attend meetings) resulted in the ouster of Bipin Chandra Pal. Although still little known to the public, Aurobindo now was in control of the policy of *Bande Mataram* and an influential voice in the councils of the party.

The 1906 session of Congress was held in Calcutta. The Extremists wanted Tilak to preside, and the Moderates were able to thwart them only by nominating Dadabhai Naoroji, the 'Grand Old Man of India', whom none could oppose. Despite this setback the Extremists were able to get most of their resolutions passed. Those on swadeshi and boycott were the most contentious. The Moderates wanted to play down the political aspect of boycott by restricting it to Bengal and to commerce. The Extremists wanted to extend it to other provinces and to other spheres of life. The inevitable clash took place in the closed-door meetings of the Subjects Committee, where all real Congress business was conducted. It was the 'most uproarious and almost rebellious session' of the committee that C. Y. Chintamani had ever seen. The Moderate journalist was pained by 'the discourtesy with which all the older leaders were greeted. . . . Intolerance was the order of the day, and the most honoured of veterans either managed to get a hearing by sheer persistence or failed to get any.'[4] When the Moderates tried to reassert their accustomed authority, Pal, Aurobindo and other Extremists walked out. Later a compromise was hammered out that satisfied most of the Extremists' demands. UP Moderate Madan Mohan Malaviya and Punjab Extremist Lala Lajpat Rai have written that Aurobindo played a significant role in these negotiations. It was his first appearance in the national political arena.

The most important resolution at Calcutta was the one concerned with the object of Congress, which never had been clearly set forth. The Bengali Extremists were the first to stress that the aim of the national movement must be the attainment of complete independence. No one articulated this better than Aurobindo. He wrote in *Bande Mataram*:

Political freedom is the life-breath of a nation; to attempt social reform, educational reform, industrial expansion, the moral improvement of the race without aiming first and foremost at political freedom, is the very height of ignorance and futility. . . . The primary requisite for national progress, national reform, is the free habit of free and healthy national thought and action which is impossible in a state of servitude.[5]

Both parties used the word swaraj, 'self-rule', in speaking of the goal of Congress; but the term was not adequately defined, and this permitted equivocation. At Calcutta the Extremists managed to pass a resolution calling for swaraj, but they were disappointed when Dadabhai Naoroji, in his famous presidential address, defined swaraj as 'self-government within the British empire'.

Despite this backsliding the Extremists generally had the better of the Moderates at Calcutta. Their success in the Subjects Committee proved that the Moderate oligarchy had lost much of its hold. After the compromise resolution on boycott was passed over the objections of Pherozshah Mehta, he commented bitterly to Tilak: 'You would not & could not have treated me so in Bombay.'[6] After Mehta had slipped away from Calcutta, an embarrassed Bhupendranath Basu apologized to the Bombay leader for 'the rudeness displayed towards you by some of our truculent and misguided youngmen', adding, 'we lose all heart when we find this sort of conduct after 22 years of the Congress in India.'[7] What was particularly disheartening to the Moderates was the thought that they, the elder statesmen of Congress, might lose control of their creation at the very moment that it was becoming effective.

At the same time the British were growing aware that the Extremists posed a genuine challenge to their rule. The predictable result was that they and the Moderates joined forces in common cause against the Extremists. G. K. Gokhale, chief spokesman of the Moderates to the government, met with Lord Minto's private secretary and expressed 'evident apprehension about the rising generation' of nationalists.[8] Meanwhile Minto himself had the pleasure of seeing Surendranath Banerjea 'sitting on my sofa with his Mahommedan opponents, asking for my assistance to moderate the evil passions of the Bengali, and inveighing against the extravagances of Bepin Chandra Pal'.[9] Politically, this sell-out was caused by the Moderates' fears that the Extremists would make the British take a hard line, delaying, perhaps indefinitely, the reforms that the Morley-Minto government had promised. Personally, it was simply the unwillingness of old veterans to let the Young Turks snatch power out of their hands.

Despite the impressive gains of the first half year of their existence the Extremists were still a minority in Congress; but they did have enthusiastic grass-roots support. In Bengal and Maharashtra the popularity of Pal and Tilak assured them of eventual supremacy. In Punjab, thanks to the efforts of Lala Lajpat Rai, their strength was growing daily. The eloquence of 'Lal-Bal-Pal', as the three chief leaders were known, was helping to give the New Party an all-India following and breaking down provincial barriers as well. After the Calcutta Congress, Tilak spent three months speaking and organizing in Bengal and the United Provinces. Pal also spoke in UP and afterwards went on a pioneering tour of the Andhra country in the politically 'backward' Madras Presidency.

Aurobindo had not fully recovered from his illness at the time of the Calcutta Congress and after the session he went to Deoghar for three months of rest. He occasionally sent in articles for *Bande Mataram* and even found time to write three acts of a verse-play, *Prince of Edur*. He thought much about the issues before the country and, immediately after returning to Calcutta, he published two series of articles that are among the most significant statements of Extremist policy ever written. One, entitled 'Shall India Be Free?', put forward the necessity of complete independence with unusual clarity and force. The other, 'The Ideal of Passive Resistance', was the first extensive public statement of an idea that, after 1919, became the principal weapon of the national movement. Passive resistance was not a new notion in India. It had been discussed even before the end of 1906, when Gandhi advanced the idea of satyagraha in South Africa. But before Aurobindo's articles no one had clearly outlined its object, methods, and limitations. As a revolutionary, Aurobindo felt that passive resistance was a subordinate means; but he did feel that legal forms of resistance such as boycott and non-co-operation could do much to prepare the ground for more active forms of revolt.

1907 was a year of unusual hardship in India. In the North, fifty lakhs died from plague. In eastern Bengal a severe drought was followed by floods that left many without shelter or food. Along with these natural disasters came social disorder. Hindu–Muslim riots broke out in Comilla, Jamalpur, and other towns in eastern Bengal. In Punjab an agrarian protest movement seemed on the verge of spreading to the army. Nothing could make the government more skittish than the prospect of a Sikh uprising. And was it not exactly fifty years since the sepoys had mutinied at Meerut? The Lieutenant-Governor of Punjab panicked, and on 6 May ordered the deportation of Lala Lajpat Rai and Ajit Singh, the two chief 'agitators' in the province. In Calcutta Aurobindo was wakened from his sleep and given the telegram bringing the bad news from Lahore. He got up, asked for pencil and paper, and wrote:

Lala Lajpatrai has been deported out of British India. The fact is its own comment. The telegram goes on to say that indignation meetings have been forbidden for four days. Indignation meetings? The hour for speeches and fine writing is past. The bureaucracy has thrown down the gauntlet. We take it up. Men of the Punjab! Race of the lion! Show these men who would stamp you into the dust that for one Lajpat they have taken away, a hundred Lajpats will arise in his place. Let them hear a hundred times louder your war-cry—*Jai Hindusthan*.[10]

In every part of the country the nationalist press was becoming bolder and more outspoken. The government responded by instituting a series of sedition prosecutions. The editors of *Vihari* (Bombay), *Punjabee* (Lahore), and several other papers were sentenced to long terms of imprisonment. In June three Calcutta journals, *Jugantar*, *Bande Mataram*, and *Sandhya*, were issued warnings. None of them moderated their tone and each was prosecuted in turn. The trial of the *Jugantar* became a cause célèbre when, at Aurobindo's suggestion, the presumed editor refused to defend himself on the grounds that British courts had no legal authority in India.

On 16 August a warrant was served against Aurobindo as editor of *Bande Mataram*. This charge had to be contested, since the party considered him too valuable to spend his time in jail. The trial made headlines around the country, bringing him for the first time to national attention. The prosecution's principal task was to prove that Aurobindo was the editor of the paper. All documents that might have established this had been discreetly destroyed. Bipin Chandra Pal, summoned to give testimony, refused to do so. In a separate trial he was sentenced to six months' imprisonment for contempt of court. In September Aurobindo was found innocent. Felicitation meetings were held across the country. His new-found celebrity did not especially please him. 'I was never ardent about fame even in my political days', he wrote years later. 'I preferred to remain behind the curtain, push people without their knowing it and get things done. It was the confounded British Government that spoiled my game by prosecuting me and forcing me to be publicly known and a "leader".'[11] The last sentence is somewhat ironic. Aurobindo would have had to come forward in any event since he now was the most important Bengali Extremist still at large. Bipin Chandra Pal was in prison in Bihar. Brahma-bandhab Upadhyay, the editor of *Sandhya*, had died in hospital while his paper was being prosecuted. As the 1907 session of Congress approached, the Extremists began looking to Aurobindo not only for written statements of policy but also for active direction of party affairs.

A British journalist has left a memorable profile of Aurobindo at the moment he took up the reins of leadership. In December 1907 H. W. Nevinson, correspondent of the *Manchester Guardian*, interviewed him at his house in Calcutta. Nevinson considered Aurobindo 'the wisest and most attractive of the Extremist leaders' on account of his uncompromising convictions. Aurobindo appeared to the Englishman to be 'a youngish man, I should think still under thirty. [He was thirty-five.] Intent dark eyes looked from his thin, clear-cut face with a gravity that seemed immovable, but the figure and bearing were those of an English graduate.' Still hardly known to the public, he yet 'inspired official circles with the greatest alarm, because his influence, though least spoken of, was most profound'. Aurobindo explained his policy to Nevinson as 'a universal Swadeshi, not limited to goods but including every phase of life'. The Extremists would 'let the Government go its way and take no notice of it at all'. A parallel Indian government would develop, possibly from the Congress framework, 'that would prepare the country for self-government'. Nevinson found in Aurobindo's tone 'a spiritual elevation', in his dedication to his country a 'concentrated vision' akin to what the non-religious call fanaticism. 'Grave with intensity, careless of fate or opinion, and one of the most silent men I have known, he was of the stuff that dreamers are made of, but dreamers who will act their dream, indifferent to the means.'[12]

The conflict between the Extremists and Moderates of Bengal came to a head at a district conference held at Midnapore on 6 December. When the local chairman betrayed his Moderate leanings by avoiding the topics of swaraj and boycott, the younger Extremists began to heckle him. The Moderates, led by the venerable Surendranath Banerjea, tried to restore order but failed. They appealed to Aurobindo to bring his party under control. When he declined to do so they called in the British police. The Extremists left the conference and, the next day, held a meeting under the chairmanship of Aurobindo. It was the first time the Bengal Extremists had met as a separate body—a portent of things to come.

Polarization was taking place in every province and at every level of the Congress organization. The national session of 1907 was scheduled to be held at Nagpur, which the Moderates considered a relatively safe locality. But Extremism was on the increase in the Central Provinces, and when preliminary meetings were held in Nagpur local Moderates had to resort to autocratic methods to remain in control. The Extremists replied with disruptive tactics and the Moderates asked for a change of venue. The central Moderate cabal, meeting secretly in the house of Pherozshah Mehta, decided that the session would be held in the thoroughly Moderate city of Surat. Extremists all over the country were outraged. Aurobindo and others wanted to secede from Congress and to hold a separate conference at Nagpur. But the majority felt, with Tilak, that the party should go to Surat and attempt to prevail. The Extremists could hold a separate conference but they should also make their presence felt in the Subjects Committee and in the open session. Aurobindo agreed to this arrangement and on 21 December he departed for Surat in a chartered train. 'The whole thousand-miles route from Kharagpur to Surat was a triumphal journey of lights, crowds, and continued cheering', wrote Barindrakumar Ghose, who accompanied his brother.

Aurobindo the new idol of the nation was hardly known then by his face, and at every small and big station a frantic crowd rushed about in the station platform looking for him in the first and second class carriages, while all the time Aurobindo sat unobserved in a third class compartment.... J. Ghosal [secretary of the Bengal Moderates] felt small in contrast and tried again and again to invite Aurobindo into his first class carriage and keep him there to save his face.[13]

At Surat there was much politicking by both parties. Each tried, by legitimate and illegitimate means, to increase the number of its delegates. The Extremists held conferences on the 24th and 25th. Aurobindo presided over both meetings. Tilak, the principal speaker, informed his listeners that the Moderates were planning to resile from the Calcutta resolutions on swadeshi, boycott, national education, and swaraj. This could not be tolerated. If retrograde resolutions were proposed the Extremists would oppose them.

One of the major issues at Surat was the election of the president of the session. The Mehta cabal had selected Rash Behari Ghose, an undistinguished Calcutta Moderate. The

Extremists wanted Ghose to step down in favour of Lala Lajpat Rai, who had just returned from his deportation. The Moderates persuaded the Punjabi leader to reject the Extremists' overtures. Outmanoeuvred, the Extremists asked Ghose to make a conciliatory gesture. He and the other Moderate leaders thought this unnecessary.

The session opened on the 26th in an atmosphere of uncertainty and tension. The opening ceremonies went off all right, but when Surendranath Banerjea tried to second the nomination of the president he was shouted down. The meeting was adjourned to the next day. On the 27th Banerjea was allowed to finish his seconding speech, but when Ghose tried to deliver his presidential address he was not given a hearing. Tilak then rose 'to move an amendment to the election of the President'. Ghose ruled him out of order. Tilak stood his ground amid rising pandemonium. A shoe whistled by him, ricocheting off Banerjea and striking Mehta. There followed the famous free-for-all that terminated the Surat session and marked the definitive break between Extremists and Moderates.

Historians still debate what actually happened at Surat. Contemporary accounts differ over almost every particular. There is controversy even over the intended target of the celebrated shoe. The really important question—who was responsible for the split?—has never been satisfactorily answered. Contemporary opinion laid the blame on Tilak. But those who knew him, Khaparde, Lajpat Rai, and Aurobindo among them, were unanimous in asserting that Tilak had no intention of splitting the Congress. Tilak himself wrote to Motilal Ghose a few weeks before the session, 'I may assure you that I or the new party, so far as I could control it, will not allow the Congress to die.'[14]

If Tilak was not responsible, who was? In 1954 a personal letter written by Sri Aurobindo two decades earlier was published in the compilation *On Himself*. In the letter Sri Aurobindo mentioned by the way: 'History very seldom records the things that were decisive but took place behind the veil; it records the show in front of the curtain. Very few people know that it was I (without consulting Tilak) who gave the order that led to the breaking of the Congress.'[15] This 'order', he made clear on another occasion, came in the form of a directive to a Maratha 'lieutenant'. Asked by this man whether his followers should break the Congress, Aurobindo replied, 'You must either swamp it or break it.'[16] Swamping proved to be impossible. The affray in the pavilion was simply the most convenient way of effecting the break. Since the posthumous publication of Sri Aurobindo's letter, many writers—among them biographers of Tilak and Lajpat Rai, and the authors of several scholarly monographs—have shown a willingness to accept Aurobindo's version.

In the same letter, Aurobindo went on to say that he was also responsible for the other decisive happening at Surat, the refusal by the Extremists 'to join the new-fangled Moderate Convention'.[17] This happened the day after the melee. The Moderates formulated a Congress 'creed' that bound subscribers to the pre-1906 Moderate programme. Some Extremists wanted to sign. Aurobindo was opposed to this on principle and he remained opposed even when Lajpat Rai informed Tilak that the government planned 'to crush the Extremists by the most ruthless repression' now that they were isolated. Tilak felt that the Extremists were not ready to face such repression. Aurobindo thought that they were, at least in Bengal and Maharashtra. Later he admitted that Tilak had been right.[18] The repression did come, with a fury that no one could have anticipated in 1907, sweeping away every important Extremist leader, Tilak and Aurobindo included.

Whether Aurobindo's intransigence helped accelerate the national movement or not is one of those historical questions that can never be satisfactorily answered. Aurobindo foresaw the possibility of collapse but he hoped that 'the repression would create a deep change in the hearts and minds of the people and the whole nation would swing over to Nationalism and the ideal of independence.'[19] This did happen, but only after the movement had been all but suspended for nearly a decade. The schism between the Moderates and Extremists lasted until 1917. Two years later Congress came out in favour of complete independence, and in 1920 it took the first steps in that direction when the non-co-operation movement was inaugurated by Mahatma Gandhi.

Between January and April 1908 various attempts were made to bring the two parties together. At the Bengal Provincial Conference, held at Pabna in February, the Moderates led by Surendranath Banerjea, and the Extremists led by Aurobindo, patched up an agreement that might have prepared the way for a wider reconciliation. But the Bombay Moderates were not interested.

On 19 April, at an all-India Moderate convention at Allahabad, the 'creed' was adopted officially as the constitution of the 'Congress'.

A *Bande Mataram* leader written by Aurobindo after the Allahabad Convention shows that his political ideals, as uncompromising as ever, were becoming more and more imbued with the 'spiritual elevation' that Nevinson had noticed. 'The sharp division' that the convention had 'created between the two parties', wrote Aurobindo,

will bring the strength of Nationalism, the sincerity of its followers and the validity of its principles to the fiercest test that any cause can undergo. Only that cause is God-created, entrusted with a mission, sure of victory which can stand by itself in a solitude, absolute and supreme, without visible shield or sword, exposed to all that the powers of the world can do to slay it, and yet survive.... God is a hard master and will not be served by halves.[20]

Nine days after this article was published, Aurobindo was arrested.

CHAPTER SIX

Waging War against the King

The Indian freedom movement achieved its aim largely through the use of non-violent means: largely, but not entirely. The popular campaigns of the twenties and thirties, which convinced the British that their position in the country was untenable, were organized and guided by a leader whose watchword was *ahimsa paramo dharmah*: non-violence is the highest law. By abjuring the use of physical force Mahatma Gandhi avoided a confrontation that would have cost many thousands of lives. The success of his strategy has made it possible, in retrospect, to minimize the contribution of India's militant revolutionaries. But they played a significant role from the beginning of the movement till its end. Although they achieved no major successes, they posed a continual challenge that the British had seriously to consider when they sat at the negotiating table.

Aurobindo was associated both with the political and the revolutionary aspects of the freedom movement. After 1906 he put most of his energy into politics; but in the beginning he gave priority to revolutionary methods, and even in the end he did not repudiate them. Sometime after 1947 he wrote:

In some quarters there is the idea that Sri Aurobindo's political standpoint was entirely pacifist, that he was opposed in principle and in practice to all violence and that he denounced terrorism, insurrection, etc., as entirely forbidden by the spirit and letter of the Hindu religion. It is even suggested that he was a forerunner of the gospel of Ahimsa. This is quite incorrect. Sri Aurobindo is neither an impotent moralist nor a weak pacifist.[1]

Aurobindo did not endorse the use of violence needlessly or for unjust ends. However the code of justice to be applied by a nation struggling for freedom was not that of the law-abiding *sattwic* man, but that of the fighter. 'The sword of the warrior is as necessary to the fulfilment of justice and righteousness as the holiness of the saint', he wrote in 1908. Which of the two was to be preferred was 'purely a matter of policy and expediency'.[2] Violent means proved inexpedient in India because the country lacked the true revolutionary temper, and because the British security forces were remarkably efficient. Aware of these difficulties, Aurobindo wrote in 1905, in what may be India's earliest statement of the policy of passive resistance:

Let the authorities remember this, that when a Government breaks the Law, by their very act the people are absolved from the obligation of obeying the Law. But let the people on their side so long as they are permitted to do so abstain from aggressive violence, let them study carefully to put their oppressors always in the wrong; but from no legitimate kind of passive resistance should they shrink.[3]

Between 1900 and 1906, while still in the Baroda service, Aurobindo tried to build up a revolutionary network in Bengal, uniting his own small group with other, somewhat older associations having varying degrees of militant orientation. He also attempted to link these groups to the secret society he had joined in Bombay in 1902. He had little success before the beginning of the anti-partition agitation, and even afterwards he was unable to bring about the 'close organization of the whole movement' that he had hoped for. 'But the movement itself did not suffer by that', he later said, 'for the general idea was taken up and activity of many separate groups led to a greater and more widespread diffusion of the revolutionary drive and its action.'[4] By March 1906, when he shifted to Bengal, a number of loosely organized groups were in operation in the province. Best established was Pramatta Nath Mitra's Anushilan Samiti, which, in the guise of a physical culture movement, had spread throughout eastern Bengal. Also active, in a less organized way, was a group led by Barindrakumar Ghose under Aurobindo's direction.

Barin was now twenty-eight. His abundant energy had so far not prevented him from failing in every activity he had ever taken up. But he seemed to have found his true vocation as a revolutionary recruiter and organizer. With just a few words he could inspire

disaffected students with the rash enthusiasm that is the revolutionary's stock-in-trade. The Bengali weekly *Jugantar*, which he and
some others had started at Aurobindo's suggestion, provided him
with a vehicle for bringing his gospel of activism to a readership
that soon numbered in the tens of thousands. Unlike *Bande
Mataram*, the vernacular *Jugantar* could openly preach revolt:

War or a revolution is an infinitely better thing than the peace under
which mortality is fast rising in India. If even fifty millions of men
disappeared from India in an attempt at deliverance, would even that not
be preferable to death in impotency and peace? Why should he who was
born a man and of a man die like a worm? Has the Almighty provided no
means of deliverance for him who cannot prove himself a man and act as
such in his life? He has. *If you cannot prove yourself a man in life, play the
man in death.* Foreigners have come and decided how you are to live. *But
how you are to die depends entirely upon yourself.** [5]

The editors of *Jugantar* went so far as to promote the formation
of 'bands' of young men who would 'direct local thought and effort
towards independence'. After providing practical tips on how to
get started, and enjoining the virtues of obedience, secrecy, etc.,
Jugantar announced: 'After the formation of a band, if we are
informed, we shall try to the best of our power to give counsel, and
to connect it with other bands.' The writer closed, with almost
insolent disdain of the authorities: 'Much inconvenience may be
felt if any letter containing the information [arrives] along with
other letters, therefore it would be greatly convenient if such
letter[s] reach the office with the aid of some persons'. [6]

Such boldness could not long go unnoticed even in a vernacular
paper. *Jugantar* was prosecuted for sedition five times in 1907 and
1908. Each time an 'editor' was imprisoned, another man took
legal responsibility for the paper and was imprisoned in his turn.
Such tactics were not without their inconveniences. After the
second prosecution Barin resolved to cut his connection with the
paper and to devote himself full-time to putting his revolutionary
ideas into practice. He and his brothers owned a garden-house on
a plot of land in the Calcutta suburb of Manicktolla. Around the

* Unfortunately *Jugantar* exists today only in the form of bad translations made
by government servants. These convey nothing of the 'rich and powerful language'
that contemporary readers admired in the original. When the British finally cracked
down on the paper, virtually every copy that had ever been printed was destroyed.
Mere possession of this organ of sedition was enough to get a man thrown into jail.

middle of 1907 Barin and a few of his young recruits (most were in their late teens or early twenties) started living at 'the Garden' on and off. For the last couple of years Barin had been thinking about starting an 'ashram' of revolutionary *sannyasis*. He had wandered through the Vindhyas searching for a suitable location, but had succeeded only in contracting a bad case of mountain-fever. His efforts to find a spiritual master to head the order were equally fruitless. Finally he decided that the Garden was as good a place as any for setting up an ashram. For the moment his friend Upendranath Banerjee would be in charge of spiritual training. He would look after practical matters.

Since 1906 Barin had been trying to supplement the secret society's resources by means of dacoities, and to create popular enthusiasm by means of assassinations. All early attempts had been failures. A plan to loot a house in Rangpur fell through, partly because some bullets (supplied, according to one account, by Aurobindo) turned out to be the wrong size for the revolver (supplied by Barin).[7] A bomb-making experiment in Deoghar ended tragically when one of Barin's recruits, a brilliant student named Prafulla Chakravarty, was killed when the bomb went off too soon. But by the end of 1907 the society's chemist, Ullaskar Dutt, was producing reliable explosives. In November the society made two unsuccessful attempts to derail the train carrying the Lieutenant-Governor of Bengal. Another attempt on 6 December 1907 came within an ace of success. The police were now alerted, but the young men went ahead with reckless abandon. By the beginning of 1908 they had turned the Garden into a small arsenal, stockpiling numerous firearms and enough explosives—it later was calculated—to blow up an entire city block.

Aurobindo was aware of what was going on at the Garden. Despite his growing absorption with political work he exercised general control over the society. Important matters of policy, such as decisions to kill officials, were usually referred to him. He was not in favour of sporadic acts of terrorism. What he wanted was a full-scale insurrection. But he did agree with Barin that successful revolutionary acts might create popular interest and at the same time intimidate the enemy. Despite his misgivings about Barin's 'childish' plots he gave at least tacit approval to them. He later explained that he did not choose to halt or redirect the society's activities because 'it is not wise to check things when they have taken a strong shape. For, something good may come out of them.'⁸

In December 1907 Barin went to the Surat Congress with the idea of linking up with revolutionaries from Maharashtra and Gujarat. He found to his surprise that no one in western India was ready to engage in revolutionary acts. He returned to Bengal convinced that it was up to him to show the way. On 11 April he sent some recruits to throw a bomb at the mayor of the French settlement of Chandernagore, who recently had prohibited a swadeshi meeting. Everything went smoothly but the bomb misfired. Barin was not unduly cast down, however, for he had already set in motion an even more daring plan.

High on the revolutionary's hit-list was an ICS officer named Douglas Kingsford, who had presided over a number of press prosecutions and other swadeshi-related trials. Hearing rumours of planned revenge, the authorities had transferred him to the remote district of Muzaffarpur in Bihar. Towards the end of February Barin's society resolved to assassinate Kingsford. Two young men, Prafulla Chaki and Khudiram Bose, were sent to do the job. The police were tipped off almost immediately, when a conspirator boasted of the plan to an infiltrator. A CID inspector went up to Muzaffarpur to investigate, but he returned when he saw no 'suspicious Bengalis'. Meanwhile Prafulla and Khudiram were studying Kingsford's habits. On the evening of 30 April they were waiting outside his bungalow at the time he usually came home from the club. A carriage drew near. Khudiram ran up with a tennis-ball-sized gelignite bomb in his hand. He threw it. His aim was perfect; the bomb went off perfectly; but it was the wrong carriage. Inside were two Englishwomen, wife and daughter of a local barrister. Both ladies were terribly injured and died soon afterwards. Khudiram was captured, tried for murder, found guilty, and executed. Prafulla got as far as the railway station at Mokameh, where he was cornered by a Bengali inspector. Rather than risk betraying the secrets of the society, he took out his revolver and shot himself. The Indian revolutionary movement had its first martyrs.

The news from Muzaffarpur reached Calcutta on the morning of 1 May. Barin thought that it might be a good idea to take a few precautions. He sent some boys to the house on Grey Street where Aurobindo was living with his wife, sister, and two members of the society. The boys removed some rifles and other materials that had been stored there. At the Garden, Barin and the others buried most of the firearms and explosives that were lying about, burned a few especially incriminating documents, and went to bed. They were wakened the next morning by an armed posse of police. All the revolutionaries were arrested, all their weapons were dug up, and boxloads of other evidence were collected and carted off to police headquarters.

At about five o'clock the same morning, Aurobindo was roused from sleep by his sister's screaming. She rushed into his room, followed by a dozen policemen brandishing revolvers. In a moment he had been arrested, bound, and handcuffed. For the next few hours he looked on as the police searched every corner of his house, carrying off, among other things, several literary notebooks, his personal letters, and a lump of clay that was found on his desk. This turned out to be not a new kind of explosive but a piece of the hut of Ramakrishna Paramhansa, which had been given Aurobindo by a monk of Ramakrishna's order.

Six other sites in Calcutta were raided at the same time, among them the society's principal bomb factory on Harrison Road. All the operations went off without a hitch. More than twenty-five men were arrested, and innumerable pieces of documentary and material evidence were collected. The accused were taken first to local *thanas*, and later to the headquarters of the detective police. All were encouraged to make confessions. In a spirit of bravado (but also with the idea of protecting his brother and others), Barin made a detailed statement in which he took full responsibility for the society's activities. Several of those arrested with him followed his example. Aurobindo made no statement and was stunned when he learnt of Barin's rash confession.

On 5 May Aurobindo and the other prisoners were produced before the Chief Presidency Magistrate in Calcutta. He transferred the case to Alipore, the headquarters of the district in which the Garden was located. Later the same day the prisoners were taken to Alipore Central Jail, on the edge of Calcutta. The charges framed against them included 'waging war against the king', the British Indian equivalent of high treason. The penalty for conviction was death by hanging.

The Alipore Bomb Trial, as it became known, was 'the first state trial of any magnitude in India', and the first in a long line of revolutionary conspiracy cases. For over a year it was the sensation of Calcutta and was closely followed by newspapers across the country. The actual trial in the sessions court was preceded by an unusually long preliminary hearing. The committing magistrate had to sift through more than 4000 documents, examine 300 or 400 material objects, and take the testimony of 277 witnesses. Arrests made after 3 May added a second batch of accused. In all thirty-three men were committed to the sessions court for trial. Here the judge was C. P. Beachcroft, ICS, who coincidentally had been at Cambridge with Aurobindo.* The fact that all of the accused persons were from 'respectable families', and that one of them was a nationally known figure of considerable attainments, added greatly to the interest of the trial.

The case against Barin and many of the others was fairly cut-and-dried. Even though those who had confessed withdrew their statements, their guilt was never really in doubt. The only question was whether they would receive the death sentence or be given a long term of imprisonment. The case against Aurobindo, on the other hand, caused the prosecution great difficulties. At the time of his arrest the Lieutenant-Governor of Bengal, convinced that he was 'the ringleader of the whole movement', but afraid that 'the facts which have been adduced are not such as would constitute clear legal proof' of guilt, urged the Government of India to deport him.[9] But the imperial government, which had been subjected to much criticism at the time of Lajpat Rai's deportation, refused to sanction Aurobindo's. 'It is infinitely preferable', wrote the Viceroy, 'that prisoners should be convicted by the ordinary law.'[10] Lord Minto's politically motivated championship of the British legal system forced the Government of Bengal to seek Aurobindo's conviction in court. It spared no expense, luring from Madras the brilliant barrister Eardley Norton to head the prosecution. Norton spent most of his time trying to establish Aurobindo's complicity. Did he know what his younger brother was up to? Certainly, said the prosecution. Not at all, said the

---

* A story made the rounds of the bar library that in the ICS entrance examination Beachcroft had stood second to Aurobindo in Greek. This was true. By a parallel irony, in the final examination Beachcroft had done better than Aurobindo in Bengali.

defence, ably led by Aurobindo's old friend C. R. Das. The prosecution was, of course, correct. Aurobindo definitely was a member of the conspiracy, albeit an inactive one. Fortunately for him, there was little solid evidence against him, though the case for the prosecution was not so weak as the government at first had feared. Among the documents found at his house was a letter from Barin to Aurobindo saying: 'We must have *sweets* all over India readymade for imergencies [*sic*].' Norton maintained that 'sweets' was a code-word for 'bombs', citing other documents where the word was used in this sense. Years later Barin admitted that the letter was just what Norton claimed it was.[11] But at the time of the trial the defence was able to throw sufficient doubt on its authenticity to make the judge 'hesitate to accept it'. Certain 'scribblings' were found in one of Aurobindo's notebooks that mentioned known revolutionaries and revolutionary acts. The judge considered this 'the most difficult point' in the case against Aurobindo, but in the end thought it insufficient to warrant conviction. Other apparently incriminating documents were produced by the prosecution, but in the end the judge found them inconclusive.[12]

The most damning evidence against Aurobindo was the testimony of Narendranath Goswami, a member of the society who had turned King's Evidence. During the hearing in the magistrate's court, Goswami said plainly that Aurobindo was the *karta* or leader of the society. His testimony would certainly have changed the complexion of the case if it had been heard in the sessions court. But before the trial began, Goswami was assassinated by two of his former comrades. His testimony, never subjected to cross examination, was invalidated.

Aurobindo spent the first month and a half of his imprisonment in solitary confinement. His cell was nine feet long and five or six feet wide. Light entered only through a barred iron door in the front. Conveniences were few. A single tin bowl had to be used for eating, drinking, bathing, gargling, and washing after defecation. This, Aurobindo wrote later, gave him an excellent opportunity for ridding himself of the sense of disgust. Although confined against his will in such an environment, he was at first not overly unhappy. 'Since I put my trust in God', he later wrote, 'I felt no loneliness there.' But after a few days without human contact he began 'to realize the enormity of solitary confinement', and 'to see why even sound and stable intellects break down during such imprisonment'. He tried to meditate, but after two or three hours 'the mind rebelled and the body became too exhausted' to continue. After suffering 'intense mental agony' he found relief in observing the world around him. Finally he realized that 'God was playing a game' with him, giving him a taste of the experience of prison and showing his mind its weakness so that he could 'get rid of it for ever'.[13] After a few days his mental disturbance ceased and he was able to pass the remainder of his imprisonment in concentrated sadhana. In Chapter 9 we will examine this critical period of Aurobindo's yogic development in more detail.

In the middle of June Aurobindo and the others were put together in a single large ward. Impressed by the boys' behaviour, the authorities felt that elaborate security measures were not required. They also hoped that closer contact between the prisoners might permit Narendranath Goswami, the informer, to obtain more information and even to persuade others to come over to the government's side. The boys proved more clever and less docile than they appeared, giving fabricated information, making plans for an escape, and smuggling messages out and revolvers in. Before the jailbreak could be staged, however, the guns were used to eliminate Goswami.

After the assassination of the informer on 31 August 1908, the prisoners were again lodged in separate cells. Aurobindo, who now was completely absorbed in his yoga, was happy to return to solitary confinement. During the two months he had spent in the large ward his meditations had been somewhat disrupted by the boys' shouting, singing, playing, and carrying on. He liked the youngsters and enjoyed talking to those who were bold enough to approach him; but he was glad to resume his practice undisturbed.

In the courtroom too Aurobindo spent most of his time meditating. Shortly after his arrest he had received an inward assurance that he would be released, and from that point on he took little interest in the proceedings. During the early stages of the trial he supplied his counsel with information and advice (which, as a former ICS probationer, he was well qualified to give); but when C. R. Das took up the case he ceased entirely to concern himself with it. Das laboured day and night, finding ways to cast doubt on the most damaging pieces of evidence. His peroration, considered a masterpiece of forensic oratory, concluded with a passage that has proved prophetic. Addressing the assessors and the judge, Das said:

My appeal to you is this: That long after this controversy is hushed in silence, long after this turmoil, this agitation ceases, long after he is dead and gone, he will be looked upon as the poet of patriotism, as the prophet of nationalism and the lover of humanity. Long after he is dead and gone his words will be echoed and re-echoed not only in India, but across distant seas and lands. Therefore I say that the man in his position is not only standing before the bar of this Court but before the bar of the High Court of History.[14]

On 6 May 1909, a year and a day after the accused were lodged in Alipore Jail, Mr Beachcroft delivered his judgment. Barindrakumar Ghose and Ullaskar Dutt were awarded the death penalty. (These sentences were later commuted to transportation for life.) Upendranath Banerjee and sixteen others received various terms of transportation and imprisonment. All the rest, Aurobindo included, were acquitted and released.

CHAPTER SEVEN

Karmayogin

After his acquittal Aurobindo went to stay in the house of his uncle, Krishna Kumar Mitra, in Calcutta. Mitra himself was not living there. He was one of nine Bengali nationalists who had been deported without trial in December 1908. These deportations were part of a concerted government campaign to crush political 'extremism' and revolutionary activism. After the Muzaffarpur bombing, and the dacoities and assassinations that followed, the authorities passed an explosives act, a newspapers act, and other measures giving the police great powers. Numerous cases were instituted against so-called revolutionary conspiracies, most of which fell through, and against nationalist newspapers, many of which resulted in convictions. In June 1908 Bal Gangadhar Tilak was put on trial for an article in which he spelled out the rationale of the Muzaffarpur killings. Found guilty of sedition, he was sentenced to six years' imprisonment in Burma. Other editors received even severer punishments, and numerous newspapers, among them *Bande Mataram* and *Jugantar*, were suppressed. Bipin Chandra Pal and Lala Lajpat Rai, the chief Extremist leaders still at liberty, fled the country and took up residence in the West. Between May 1909 and February 1910, when the deportees were set free, Aurobindo was the only important Bengali Extremist, indeed the only Extremist with a countrywide reputation, in a position to lead a party that had become disorganized, demoralized and inactive. This circumstance drew him quickly back into politics.

In June Aurobindo started an English newspaper, *Karmayogin*, 'a Weekly Review of National Religion, Literature, Science, Philosophy, &c.' In it he published, along with political comment,

articles on Vedanta and Kalidasa's poetry, translations of the
Upanishads and Bankim's novel *Anandamath*, and studies of
hypnosis, Indian painting, and a wide variety of other subjects.
Practically all the paper's editorial contents, three to eight large
pages each week, were written by Aurobindo. He was able to
produce so much because he worked from a 'yogic state': the
creative energy, he said, 'used to run down to my hand while
writing'.[1] In August he doubled his load by starting a Bengali
weekly, *Dharma*. He had now sufficient mastery over the language
to write most of *Dharma*'s articles himself. Like *Karmayogin*,
Dharma ranged far beyond the confines of contemporary politics.
In its columns Aurobindo published a commentary on the Gita,
articles on other Indian scriptures, essays on nationalism and
religion, art criticism, and a story.

The declared purpose of *Karmayogin* was to assist an 'increasing
tendency' for the two main streams of India's national life, religion
and politics, 'to unite again into one mighty invincible and grand-
iose flood'. In old India no line was drawn between the two: 'the
life of the nation ... flowed in a broad and single stream'. But,
since the time of the British conquest, Indian politics had 'crept in
a channel cut for it by European or Europeanised minds'. Indians
were expected to observe the distinction drawn in Europe between
religion and every other aspect of life. In the European view,
wrote Aurobindo, who knew his subject well, religion was 'all very
well in its place, but it has nothing to do with politics or science or
commerce, which it spoils by its intrusion; it is meant only for
Sundays'. The European believed that all the problems of existence could be solved by political and social machinery. 'He seeks
to renovate humanity by schemes of society and systems of government; he hopes to bring about the millennium by an act of
Parliament.' Aurobindo rejected this mechanistic approach to life:

The task we set before ourselves is not mechanical but moral and spiritual.
We aim not at the alteration of a form of government but at the building
up of a nation. Of that task politics is a part, but only a part. We shall
devote ourselves not to politics alone, nor to social questions alone, nor to
theology or philosophy or literature or science by themselves, but we
include all these in one entity which we believe to be all-important, the
dharma, the national religion which we also believe to be universal. . . . To
understand the heart of this *dharma*, to experience it as a truth, to feel the
high emotions to which it rises and to express and execute it in life is what

we understand by Karmayoga. We believe that it is to make the *yoga* the ideal of human life that India rises today; by the *yoga* she will get the strength to realize her freedom, unity and greatness, by the *yoga* she will keep the strength to preserve it.[2]

Two terms in this passage require elucidation: dharma, specifically the *sanatana dharma* or 'eternal religion', and yoga, specifically *karmayoga*, the 'yoga of action'. Properly understood, they cast light on all of Aurobindo's thought and action during this period. The dharma or 'religion' that he put forward was not popular Hinduism, but rather 'the religion which embraces Science and faith, Theism, Christianity, Mahommedanism and Buddhism and yet is none of these'. If at this time he gave it the name of Hinduism, it was 'only because the Hindu nation has kept' this universal religion better than others. But, being universal, it was 'not circumscribed by the confines of a single country'.[3]

'Hinduism', the term used in modern times to refer to the Indian religious tradition, was for Aurobindo, at the time under study, simply a convenient term for the eternal religion (sanatana dharma) that transcended all sectarian definition.* The 'wider Hinduism' he endorsed was not confined to any form of religion current in India or elsewhere. It had, he wrote, 'many scriptures, Veda, Vedanta, Gita, Upanishad, Darshana, Purana, Tantra, nor could it reject the Bible or the Koran; but its real, most authoritative scripture is in the heart in which the Eternal has His dwelling'.[4]

To Aurobindo this eternal religion was nothing if its fundamental truths could not be experienced. The greatness of universal 'Hinduism' was that it was 'the one religion which impresses on mankind the closeness of God to us and embraces in its compass all the possible means by which man can approach God'.[5] It was founded not on doctrine but on spiritual experiences that could be attained through practice of the discipline known in India as yoga. There are many paths of yoga; the one Aurobindo was principally concerned with at this time was karmayoga, 'the application of Vedanta and Yoga to life'. To those who said that one had to renounce life to practice yoga, Aurobindo replied: 'the spiritual

---

* It should be remembered that 'Hinduism' is the anglicization of a Persian term that in its origin was geographical and not sectarian. What non-Indians called 'Hinduism' was known to those who practiced it simply as dharma or sanatana dharma.

life finds its most potent expression in the man who lives the
ordinary life of men in the strength of the Yoga and under the law
of the Vedanta.'[6] The converse also was true: the activities of the
ordinary life, politics included, became most effective when
infused with energy from a spiritual source. Men achieved greatness in their appointed fields when they became 'serviceable and
specially-forged instruments of the Power which determines
them'. This was true even if the instrument was unaware of the
source of his strength, as were, for example, Mirabeau and
Napoleon.[7] The yogin on the path of works, the karmayogin, was
to a greater or lesser degree a conscious instrument: 'he experiences the advent of knowledge and feels himself passive and the
divine force working unresisted through his mind, his speech, his
senses and all his organs'.[8]

Since January 1908, when he had a series of powerful spiritual
experiences,* Aurobindo had felt himself to be such an instrument. In a speech he delivered in Nasik later that month, he said:
'Whatever I do is not done by me of my own accord. My actions
are dictated by God. I am simply an instrument in His hands.'[9]
Such an attitude is not without its dangers. An insincere
'instrument' can easily proclaim that he is following an inner
guidance when in fact he is simply satisfying his desires or fulfilling
his ambitions. Or the instrument may be fundamentally sincere
but misled by false guidance; for if there are helpful divine forces
there are also anti-divine *asuric* forces ready to waylay the unwary.
Even if one avoids these pitfalls, there is still much room for error.
Relying on his inner guidance, Aurobindo was led into 'many
mistakes. For days and days together', he related in 1939, 'I would
follow wrong lines and come to know only at the end that it was all
a mistake.' But he said also that 'when you don't listen' to the
inner voice, 'bad results' follow.[10] He had to develop a sort of inner
tact—something many would-be yogins never acquire. Some fall
instead into 'a kind of megalomania', justifying myriad errors with
the formula: 'I, I am *the* instrument—how great an instrument I
am—through me all will be done.'[11] Aurobindo attributed his
success in negotiating these hazards to two complementary qualities. First, he followed the inner guidance implicitly, and not only
so far as it agreed with his desires or preconceived notions.

* These will be discussed in detail in Chapter 9.

Secondly, he never lost his capacity for critical self-appraisal.

The writing of *Karmayogin* and *Dharma* was only part of Auro-bindo's action-in-yoga. As the leader of the Extremist party, he delivered more than ten speeches between May and October. A contemporary has written that wherever he went 'he was greeted with fervent and affectionate enthusiasm'.[12] This was true at least of the first part of the period. On 30 May he was invited to Uttarpara, a town not far from Calcutta, where he gave his most celebrated speech. Asked to talk on Hinduism, he presented the essence of the ideas he would later develop in *Karmayogin*:

We speak often of the Hindu religion, of the Sanatan Dharma, but few of us really know what that religion is. Other religions are preponderatingly religions of faith and profession, but the Sanatan Dharma is life itself; it is a thing that has not so much to be believed as lived. This is the Dharma that for the salvation of humanity was cherished in the seclusion of this peninsula from of old. It is to give this religion that India is rising. She does not rise as other countries do, for self or when she is strong, to trample on the weak. She is rising to shed the eternal light entrusted to her over the world. India has always existed for humanity and not for herself and it is for humanity and not for herself that she must be great.[13]

Through June and most of July Aurobindo spoke practically every week, either in Calcutta and its environs or in the districts. His speeches were concerned mostly with current politics, but sometimes they transcended their immediate context. Comment-ing on the government's campaign against the Extremists at the Barisal District Conference on 19 June, he said: 'Repression is nothing but the hammer of God that is beating us into shape so that we may be moulded into a mighty nation and an instrument for his work in the world. We are iron upon his anvil and the blows are showering upon us not to destroy but to re-create. Without suffering there can be no growth.'[14] Unfortunately the metal proved too brittle to bear the continual blows of persecution. After August the enthusiasm that his release had rekindled died down, and Aurobindo found himself addressing not thousands but a hundred or less—and these mostly passers-by. This experience gave him 'a good insight into our people's psychology'.[15]

One group never ceased to take interest in Aurobindo's speeches—the British police. From the moment of his acquittal, the government had been looking for a way to put him back in jail. During the summer and autumn of 1909 his writings and speeches were among the only significant expressions of nationalist sentiment in the country. As his influence grew, the provincial governments of Bengal and the imperial government of India regarded him with increasing anxiety. The Chief Secretary of the Government of Bengal wrote of him as 'the most dangerous of our adversaries now at large'. The same epithet was used by the Lieutenant-Governors of Bengal and Eastern Bengal and Assam, and later also by the Viceroy, who referred to him as 'the most dangerous man we have to deal with at present'.[16] During the middle of 1909, different departments of the government launched a three-pronged offensive against him. The object was to remove him from the scene by means of appeal, deportation or arrest.

The simplest way to return Aurobindo to jail would have been to convict him, on appeal, for the crimes he had been acquitted of at Alipore. Immediately after his release the Government of Bengal consulted legal experts, one of whom was of the opinion that there was 'a fair chance of a conviction against Arabindo Ghose being obtained in appeal'. This was not sufficiently encouraging. An unsuccessful appeal would have enhanced his reputation as a suffering patriot and increased anti-government feeling. On 18 August Sir Edward Baker, Lieutenant-Governor of Bengal, vetoed the idea of an appeal.[17]

Less than a fortnight later, Baker had to consider another proposal, this one emanating from the imperial government. On 6 July Sir Harold Stuart, Chief Secretary of the Government of India, wrote to his counterpart in the Bengal secretariat: 'I would not hesitate to deport Arabindo [sic] if he cannot be silenced in any other way. If he is allowed to go on he will very soon have the country in a blaze again.'[18] The advantage of deportation was that it sidestepped the judicial process. The statute under which Lala Lajpat Rai and others had been deported allowed the government to suspend habeas corpus, placing an individual 'against whom there may not be sufficient ground to institute judicial proceedings . . . under restraint', confining him 'to a fortress, jail or other place' anywhere in the empire. But the Government of Bengal was not anxious to make use of this statute in mid 1909. The jails and fortresses of north India and Burma already held nine Bengali leaders whose continued detention provoked almost daily comment in the Indian and British press, as well as an occasional question in Parliament. Baker was unwilling to lay himself open to more of such criticism. He gave the proposal to deport Aurobindo lengthy consideration, but ultimately rejected it.[19]

The Lieutenant-Governor believed that the best way to deal with Aurobindo would be to prosecute him for an indictable offence such as sedition. Instructions were issued to the police, who combed each issue of the *Karmayogin* in the hope of finding an incautious statement. They found none. During his years as editor of *Bande Mataram* Aurobindo had mastered the art of keeping his writings, however incendiary, within the letter of the law. The police also made shorthand transcriptions of all his speeches and went over them word by word. A few of his remarks seemed to come close to sedition, but none of them actually crossed the line. By the end of July the government had to admit that it had no case against Aurobindo. For the moment he was safe from arrest.[20]

During this period Aurobindo was not only the Extremists' chief public spokesman but also their principal policy-maker and negotiator. In September he led the party at the Provincial Conference at Hooghly, the most important political meeting in Bengal in 1909. The split between Moderates and Extremists was not so profound in Bengal as elsewhere, and there was some hope that the two parties might be able to patch up their differences. This might have opened the way for the Extremists to take part in national Congress politics. Aurobindo was himself not inclined to treat with the Moderates; but many in his party wanted union and he did not stand in their way.

In the event, union proved impossible. The central Moderate body required Extremists to sign the 'creed' that had been formulated at Surat. Aurobindo refused to do so. As a politician he could be extremely obstinate. At one point in the negotiations Surendranath Banerjea, the Moderate leader, suggested that Aurobindo and others attend an important conference as Moderates, since as Extremists they would be excluded. Many in the party were in favour of going, but Aurobindo 'just said "No"', and the negotiations fell through.[21] He was willing to compromise but was not prepared to renounce fundamental principles. At the Hooghly Conference there was a debate over the number of Extremists and Moderates to be included in the Calcutta delegation of the Subjects Committee. The Moderates wanted ten from their party as against five Extremists. Aurobindo suggested eight

Moderates and seven Extremists. Neither side gave way and there was a deadlock. Eventually, according to the report of a police informer, Aurobindo 'suggested, as a compromise, the appointment of six nationalists [Extremists] and nine moderates, and this was agreed to'.[22]

Such give and take is the ordinary stuff of politics. The incident, hardly significant in itself, takes on interest when it is recalled that at this time Aurobindo was deeply involved in yoga. A diary he kept in July shows that his sadhana went on undisturbed even during a busy political tour. That he could still give importance to so mundane a detail as whether six or seven Extremists should attend a meeting can be taken as a positive indication that his yoga was not divorced from life. Certainly he did not need an anchorite's cave for his practice. Many years later he wrote to a disciple who complained of having poor conditions for meditation: 'As for concentration and perfection of the being and the finding of the inner self, I did as much of it walking in the streets of Calcutta to my work or in duty with men during my work as alone and in solitude.'[23]

A few days after the Hooghly Conference, Aurobindo went to Sylhet in north-eastern Bengal to attend a local party meeting. Back in Calcutta by the beginning of October, he delivered the ill-attended speeches and conducted the unfruitful parleys that have been mentioned above. In December, after the final failure of the Extremist-Moderate negotiations, he issued a major policy statement in *Karmayogin* under the heading 'To My Countrymen'. In this article he condemned the Moderates for rejecting the Extremists' hand of fellowship, and criticized the government for deluding the country with the sham reforms of the Indian Councils Act (Morley-Minto Reforms). These, he said, gave no real concessions to Indian nationalism and upset the communal balance by introducing separate electorates for Muslims. He called on his party to assume once more 'their legitimate place in the struggle for Indian liberties'. The Extremists' goal, he stated, was 'the perfect self-fulfillment of India and the independence which is the condition of self-fulfillment'. In order to achieve this, 'the first requisite' was 'the organisation of the Nationalist [Extremist] Party'. He proposed holding a meeting of the Nationalist Council (a parallel National Congress) early in 1910.[24] Before these plans could be carried out, however, the political climate of the country changed dramatically for the worse.

In January, revolutionaries indirectly connected with Aurobindo assassinated a police official in the Calcutta High Court. In
retaliation the Bengal administration took steps to crush the
nationalist movement once and for all. The government of Sir
Edward Baker, which five months earlier had been unwilling to
deport Aurobindo alone, now put his name on a list of fifty-three
Bengali nationalists whose immediate deportation it recommended. The Government of India rejected Bengal's proposal; at the
same time, however, India prodded the provincial government to
bring a sedition case against Aurobindo for 'To My Countrymen'.
Bengal was less than anxious to take responsibility for instituting a
prosecution. Through February and March it studied the merits of
the case, finally deciding to act early in April. An arrest warrant
was issued but could not be served, for Aurobindo had left the
province.

One evening in mid February, Aurobindo was informed that the
next day the *Karmayogin* office would be searched and he
arrested. 'While considering what should be his attitude,' he wrote
years later, 'he received a sudden command from above to go to
Chandernagore in French India. He obeyed the command at once,
for it was now his rule to move only as he was moved by the divine
guidance and never to resist and depart from it; . . . in ten minutes
[he] was at the river *ghat* and in a boat plying on the Ganges; in a
few hours he was at Chandernagore where he went into secret
residence.'[25]

Chandernagore, a town twenty miles up the Ganges from Calcutta, was under French administration. So long as Aurobindo
stayed there, he was safe from British arrest. Nevertheless,
he remained in seclusion in houses arranged for by Motilal
Roy, a member of the local revolutionary network. After about a
month in Chandernagore, Aurobindo received a second *adesh*
(command) telling him to go to Pondicherry, another French
enclave situated a hundred miles south of Madras. Between Chandernagore and Pondicherry lay more than a thousand miles of
territory controlled by the British. Elaborate arrangements had to
be made for his passage. On the night of 31 March he was taken by
boat to Calcutta and placed on a French ship that departed the
next day. On 4 April 1910 he arrived in Pondicherry, where he was
received and housed by Tamil nationalists.

Aurobindo's departure from Calcutta in February 1910 marked the end of his active participation in the Indian freedom movement. The warrant against him was withdrawn in November when 'To My Countrymen' was found not seditious by the Calcutta High Court. From that time forward, with the possible exception of the years of the First World War, he could have returned to British India without fear of arrest. He elected not to do so for reasons unconnected with politics. The success of the freedom movement now seemed to him to be assured. In a newspaper interview of January 1910 he had predicted that 'Britain would be compelled by pressure of Indian resistance and the pressure of international events to concede independence.' Therefore, he felt, 'his own personal intervention' was 'no longer indispensable'.[26] The work that demanded his attention was not political but spiritual.

Since his release from Alipore jail, Aurobindo's 'inner spiritual life' had been 'pressing upon him for an exclusive concentration'.[27] Once settled in Pondicherry he could give this his full attention, free from the demands of his friends and the harassment of his enemies. In a letter of 1911 he wrote that he had resolved to retire briefly in order to 'complete my Yoga unassailed'.[28] He originally thought that this would take him a year or two at most. But before long 'the magnitude of the spiritual work set before him became more and more clear to him, and he saw that the concentration of all his energies on it was necessary.' The two years extended to four, then ten, then twenty. Never during this period did he abandon his intention of returning to the field of action; but his idea of the relation between action and yoga underwent a fundamental change. He had begun his sadhana with the idea of getting power and guidance to help him in his work. Now he began to look on the work as 'a part and result' of his sadhana. The scope of the work envisaged also changed. Hitherto limited to 'the service and liberation of the country', it now 'fixed itself in an aim, previously only glimpsed, which was world-wide in its bearing and concerned with the whole future of humanity'.[29]

During his first few years in Pondicherry Aurobindo kept in contact with the Bengal revolutionaries through Motilal Roy and others. For many more years he remained a role-model and inspiration to the country's youth. As late as 1920, wrote Subhas Chandra Bose, Aurobindo remained 'easily the most popular leader in Bengal, despite his voluntary exile'.[30] But many of

Aurobindo's admirers became disillusioned when he remained in retirement even after Congress adopted complete independence as its goal (two decades after he and his associates had first put it forward) and began to take positive steps towards its achievement. Among the disillusioned was Jawaharlal Nehru, who wrote in 1962: 'When Gandhiji started his non-co-operation movements and convulsed India, we expected Sri Aurobindo to emerge from his retirement and join the great struggle. We were disappointed at his not doing so.'[31]

The disappointment felt by Nehru and others has coloured the judgement of many historians of the freedom movement. The tendency now is to look on Aurobindo as an inspiring writer and ideologue, but to discount his practical work between 1906 and 1910. More detailed study of this period may lead to a reappraisal of his contribution. But to obtain a just estimate of his political activities it is necessary to understand that Aurobindo, the karma-yogin, saw no essential difference between work and sadhana. His actions were the outward expression of his yoga. In 1909 he obeyed an inner direction to revive the national movement even after achieving a yogic realization that typically leads to the renunciation of action. In 1910 he received an adesh that directed him to leave Bengal. He obeyed this command that led to his retirement from politics, even as earlier he had obeyed the command to engage in it.

Part Two

CHAPTER EIGHT

Early Years in Pondicherry

Pondicherry, where Sri Aurobindo arrived on 4 April 1910,* was one of five remnants of France's failed Indian empire, a coastal pocket little larger than the town where most of its Tamil-speaking population lived. Once vibrant with the ambitions of Robert Clive's rival Joseph François Dupleix, it had become, in the words of a contemporary French visitor, 'a dead city that had been something and remembers it, rigid in its dignity, irreproachably correct, concealing beneath an impeccable coat of whitewash the cracks in the old walls'.[1] The town had few pretensions to culture. It was better known for smuggling than legitimate trade. The most notable result of its democratic elections was that every four years the streets were taken over by *goondas* in the pay of one or another faction.

Viewed in retrospect, the most significant group in Pondicherry in 1910, politically as well as culturally, was a small band of nationalists living in exile from British India. First to arrive were Subramania Bharati and S. N. Tirumalachari, the editor and the owner respectively of the Tamil newspaper *India*. After the government press crackdown of 1908, these two had fled from Madras and begun bringing out the paper from Pondicherry. Bharati remained for almost a decade, writing, besides political journalism, many of the poems that have won him the reputation as the greatest modern Tamil poet. In time the *India* office developed into the centre of the most active group of Extremists in southern

* Just as in Part 1 I referred consistently to the subject of this biography as Aurobindo, though he did not adopt this spelling until 1906, so in this part I will refer to him consistently as Sri Aurobindo, though this appellation did not come into use until 1926.

India. One of them was V. V. S. Aiyar, a former member of the Paris-based revolutionary organization led by Shamji Krishna-varma and Madame Cama, and an accomplished Tamil scholar as well. The arrival of Sri Aurobindo added a new dimension to the town's political and cultural life. Even in retirement he remained a major influence on the freedom movement and, despite his growing absorption in yoga, he produced during his Pondicherry years a large and varied body of literature. Around him gathered a circle of young Bengali nationalists, some of whom contributed to the cultural efflorescence of their adopted home.

These outstanding political and literary figures, along with others of more modest attainments, had settled in Pondicherry because it offered them freedom from harassment by the British. At the beginning of the century there was more rivalry than co-operation between British and French imperialism. The *entente cordiale* was still in its infancy, and the French were glad to give asylum to refugees from British India, if only to nettle their rivals.

When Sri Aurobindo reached Pondicherry he was met by two members of the *India*-office group and taken to the house of Shankara Chettiar, a businessman with nationalist sympathies. Sri Aurobindo remained in Chettiar's house in almost complete seclusion for six months. With him were Bijoy Nag, who had accompanied him on the ship from Calcutta, and Suresh Chakravarty (Moni), who had gone ahead to make arrangements for his stay. Later in the year they were joined by Saurin Bose, a cousin of Sri Aurobindo's wife Mrinalini, and Nolini Kanta Gupta, who like Bijoy had stood trial with Sri Aurobindo at Alipore. The five lived very frugally. What little money they had came from old friends in Bengal and Baroda, and new friends in the Madras Presidency. These contributions were limited and irregular, and Sri Aurobindo was often in an embarrassed condition. In July 1912 he wrote to Motilal Roy in Chandernagore, 'The situation just now is that we have Rs. 1½ or so in hand.'[2] In another letter of the same period he spelled out the problem in more detail: 'At present, I am at the height of my difficulties, in debt, with no money for the morrow, besieged in Pondicherry and all who could help are in temporary or permanent difficulties.' He looked forward to a time when he would be able to 'create means', but for the moment was constrained to ask for enough money to get him through the next two months. As a yogin he left such matters to the Divine, but this did not prevent him from commenting, with characteristic humour: 'No doubt, God will provide, but He has contracted a bad habit of waiting till the last moment.'[3] Later his sources of support became more dependable, and eventually he was able to 'create means' by publishing his writings.

On 7 November 1910, the day that the case against the *Karmayogin* was dismissed, Sri Aurobindo wrote to the editor of the *Hindu*, a leading paper of Madras, announcing that he was living in Pondicherry 'as a religious recluse' and adding that he wished to 'see and correspond with no one in connection with political subjects'.[4] The letter seems to have had the opposite of its intended effect. Sri Aurobindo's assertion that he wished 'to pursue his Yogic sadhana undisturbed' did not deter scores of would-be disciples from flocking to see him. He had no desire to become a guru. Writing again to the *Hindu* in February 1911 he complained in mock despair:

I find myself besieged by devotees who insist on seeing me whether I will or not. They have crossed all India to see me—from Karachi's waters, from the rivers of the Punjab, whence do they not come? They only wish to stand at a distance and get mukti by gazing on my face; or they will sit at my feet, live with me wherever I am or follow me to whatever lands. They clamber on to my windows to see me or loiter and write letters from neighbouring Police stations. I wish to inform all future pilgrims of the kind that their journey will be in vain.[5]

Sri Aurobindo did not even treat the four youths who lived with him as disciples. He meditated and read the Vedas and wrote philosophy; they shopped and did a bit of housework and roamed about the town. Nolini and Moni also spent some time studying and writing. Sri Aurobindo taught them Greek, Latin and French, and encouraged them in their literary efforts. Eventually they became fairly well known as writers of Bengali. In Pondicherry, however, their fame rested chiefly upon their skill as football players, Nolini excelling as a right wing and Moni as a left out. Sri Aurobindo never suggested they spend their time in more edifying pursuits.

Partly as a result of their financial ups and downs, Sri Aurobindo and his companions had to shift house three times between 1910 and 1913. In October of that year they were able to rent a 'decent house' on Rue François Martin, near the centre of town. The building was large and airy but conditions remained primitive. All bathed under an open tap in the yard and dried themselves with a single towel. Soap was a luxury indulged in every fourth day. Occasionally Sri Aurobindo had to go without footwear. Clothing was so scarce that the manager of the household once added this note to one of Sri Aurobindo's letters: 'We are in absolute want of clothes. Will you please pay a little attention to that point and relieve us from this absolute want?'[6] Meals were simple and often badly prepared. Sri Aurobindo ate whatever was put before him, without comment. If anyone criticized the food, saying, for example, that the meat lacked salt, he just remarked, 'Yes, there is no salt', and continued eating. He used to say that one could find *rasa* even in badly cooked and tasteless food. Dietary regulations did not interest him. He regularly ate meat and drank wine, which in French Pondicherry was easily obtainable and cheap. Some years later he wrote in his principal book on yoga, 'We must not . . . imagine that the purity of the mind depends on the things we eat or drink.' He did concede, however, that 'during a certain stage restrictions in eating and drinking are useful to our inner progress'.[7] Later in life he adopted a vegetarian diet, foreswore even an occasional glass of wine, and abandoned two other long-standing habits—smoking and tea-drinking. The renunciation of meat, alcohol and tobacco were institutionalized when his household became an ashram in the late 1920s, but he never ceased to look on such things as secondary matters in the spiritual life.

Sri Aurobindo's abstemious eating habits helped him to keep in good health. He spent most of his time indoors but was careful to give his body sufficient exercise. Walking briskly up and down in his rooms, sometimes for as much as ten hours a day, he created a channel a foot wide and two inches deep in the soft floor. His activities were largely intellectual, but he trained himself to do physical work and performed it regularly. At one point it was his duty to cook fish for the cats that had colonized his house.

At the beginning of his stay in Pondicherry Sri Aurobindo tried to keep his presence secret from the British. Despite his precautions they learned quickly that he was in French India, and began a surveillance of his activities that lasted for twenty-seven years. The Madras office of the Criminal Investigation Department (CID) maintained a large contingent of plainclothesmen to keep watch over him and the other nationalists. These spies created an atmosphere of intrigue and tension in the town. Local hooligans, tempted by British money, tried to abduct V. V. S. Aiyar, and at one point were rumoured to be plotting to do the same to Sri Aurobindo. When reports of this reached Nolini and the others, they armed themselves with bottles of acid and patrolled the house at night. Later a dishonest local resident lodged a complaint against the revolutionaries, having first gone to the trouble of planting incriminatory documents on the property of V. V. S. Aiyar. Fortunately these were discovered and shown to be forgeries before the French police could investigate. Soon afterwards the *juge d'instruction* (examining magistrate) paid a call on Sri Aurobindo. His visit was brief and cordial. Noticing copies of Latin and Greek texts on Sri Aurobindo's table, the official exclaimed, *'Il sait du latin, il sait du grec!'* ('He knows Latin! He knows Greek!') Apologizing for his intrusion, he politely took his leave. The Pondicherry government's admiration for the scholar in their midst caused them to ignore the hostile pressure of the British until 1914. During the War, however, the situation changed, because the British were helping to hold back the Germans in France and Belgium. At one point the Governor of Pondicherry hinted that it might be best for the refugees to go voluntarily to Africa, otherwise he might have to deport them. At a meeting at Sri Aurobindo's house Subramania Bharati said that he was ready to go to Algiers. Sri Aurobindo heard him out, then said: 'Mr Bharati, I am not going to budge an inch from Pondicherry. I know nothing will happen to me. As for yourself, you can do what you like.'[8] This storm blew over, and the refugees remained in the town unmolested. After the War their position became less precarious but they never were able to take their security for granted.

The British may have been unable to touch Sri Aurobindo, but they could make things difficult for those who came to see him. In 1912 D. L. Purohit, an acquaintance of Sri Aurobindo's from Baroda, paid him an hour's visit and as a result lost his job. The previous year Alexandra David-Néel, a French writer and traveller renowned as the first European woman to enter Tibet, spent an afternoon 'reviewing the ancient philosophical ideas of India' with Sri Aurobindo. Impressed by his 'rare intelligence', she wrote in a letter to her husband, 'he speaks with such clarity, there is such lucidness in his reasoning, such lustre in his eyes, that he leaves one with the impression of having contemplated the genius of India such as one dreams it to be after reading the noblest pages of Hindu philosophy.'⁹ With these impressions still fresh in her mind, Mme David-Néel arrived in Madras, where she was met by the chief of the local CID. When the lady explained that she was interested in Sri Aurobindo only as a philosopher, the official replied, 'He certainly is a very remarkable scholar, but he is a dangerous man. We hold him responsible for the recent assassination of Mr Ashe.' Ashe, a British collector, had been killed by a revolutionary acting under the orders of V. V. S. Aiyar. Such incidents made the British unwilling to relax their surveillance of Sri Aurobindo, however much he distanced himself from politics.

Mme David-Néel had heard of Sri Aurobindo from her Parisian friends Paul and Mirra Richard. Paul Richard, a lawyer and supporter of philanthropic causes, had come to Pondicherry in 1910 in connection with the French elections. He also had some interest in spiritual matters, owing largely to the influence of his future wife Mirra, a student of occultism and an advanced practitioner of the Western equivalent of yoga. When Richard heard that a yogin named Aurobindo Ghose was living in Pondicherry, he asked to be introduced to him. Sri Aurobindo consented and the two had an extended conversation. Richard went away from the meeting convinced that Sri Aurobindo was the spiritual master that he and Mirra had been searching for.

In 1914 Richard again came to Pondicherry, this time accompanied by his wife. The Frenchman suggested that he and Sri Aurobindo bring out a review in which they could present the philosophical synthesis that they had discussed. Sri Aurobindo agreed, and on 15 August 1914, his forty-second birthday, the first issue of *Arya* appeared. Six months later, Richard was called away to the War. Sri Aurobindo carried on alone until 1920, each month writing and publishing a sixty-four-page issue of the journal. A reader unacquainted with the process of publication may have difficulty appreciating what this meant. Every year Sri Aurobindo produced from scratch the equivalent of two or three full-length books, writing and revising all the matter, seeing it through the press, correcting proofs, and even doing some of the office work. In six and a half years, under a continual deadline, he wrote all of the works upon which his reputation as a philosopher, Sanskrit scholar, political scientist and literary critic is based. Regarded simply as intellectual and physical labour, it was an extraordinary achievement.

While writing and editing the *Arya*, Sri Aurobindo lived quietly in the house on Rue François Martin with a varying number of companions. One of them was Amrita, a young man of Pondicherry who had become part of the household. Amrita relates that during this period Sri Aurobindo used to guide his life by one or another ruling idea. For some time it was democracy. The slogan of the French Revolution, *liberté, égalité, fraternité,* became Sri Aurobindo's watchword. When Amrita gave a drunken compositor a dressing down, Sri Aurobindo told him not to meddle in the man's affairs. The compositor was free to drink as much as he liked. Amrita simply should tell him to honour the terms of his contract. Later, when service to humanity became Sri Aurobindo's central idea, he asked Amrita not to carry the *Arya* proofs up to his room. 'Why do you bring them here?,' he asked. 'It is my duty to take them. I am not old. I must do my work.' The young men, who were beginning to look on Sri Aurobindo as their spiritual master, found such egalitarian behavior a little odd. It was a strange sort of guru who requested permission to enter one's room, or who said 'I beg your pardon' if his foot accidentally touched another's.

During the *Arya* period, spiritual relations gradually developed between Sri Aurobindo and the young men gathered around him. At the same time he was letting his family connections lapse. He corresponded with none of his relatives and only occasionally wrote to his wife. Mrinalini had been living with her father since Sri Aurobindo's departure from Calcutta. He intended to bring her to Pondicherry when conditions permitted, but in 1918, while she was getting ready to come, she died in the great influenza epidemic. Sri Aurobindo was never noted for displays of emotion. It is said, however, that when he read the telegram informing him of his wife's death, his eyes filled with tears. A letter he wrote to his father-in-law at this time shows that his affection for Mrinalini was sincere and profound:

I have not written to you with regard to this fatal event in both our lives: words are useless in face of the feelings it has caused, if even they can ever express our deepest emotions. God has seen good to lay upon me the one sorrow that could still touch me to the centre. He knows better than ourselves what is best for each of us, and now that the first sense of the irreparable has passed, I can bow with submission to his divine purpose. The physical tie between us is, as you say, severed; but the tie of affection subsists for me. Where I have once loved, I do not cease from loving.[10]

Nineteen-twenty was a pivotal year for the Indian freedom movement. Lokamanya Tilak died on 1 August, the same day that Mahatma Gandhi's non-co-operation movement began. Twice during this year Sri Aurobindo was offered positions that would have enabled him to influence nationalist policy. He rejected both offers. The letters in which he gave his reasons for doing so illustrate his current way of looking at the relationship between yoga and action in the world.

In January Joseph Baptista, an associate of Tilak's, asked Sri Aurobindo to become editor of the printed organ of a new party that Tilak and others had founded. Sri Aurobindo replied that he was not the right man for the job because, 'as the editor of your paper, I should be bound to voice the opinion of others and reserve my own, and while I have full sympathy with the general ideas of the advanced parties . . . I am almost incapable of limiting myself in that way, at least to the extent that would be requisite.' He affirmed his continuing interest in the national movement, but explained that he no longer gave political action the priority he once did:

I do not at all look down on politics or political action or consider I have got above them. I have always laid a dominant stress and I now lay an entire stress on the spiritual life, but my idea of spirituality has nothing to do with ascetic withdrawal or contempt or disgust of secular things. There is to me nothing secular, all human activity is for me a thing to be included in a complete spiritual life, and the importance of politics at the present time is very great. But my line and intention of political activity would differ considerably from anything now current in the field.[11]

During the period of his involvement in politics Sri Aurobindo had had one single aim: 'to get into the mind of the people a settled will for freedom and the necessity of the struggle to achieve it'. This aim, he said, had been achieved. 'The will to self-determination, if the country keeps its present temper, as I have no doubt it will, is bound to prevail before long. What preoccupies me now is the question of what it is going to do with its self-determination, how will it use its freedom, on what lines is it going to determine its future?'

Twenty-seven years before the attainment of independence Sri Aurobindo was already looking ahead to one of the great questions that has faced India since 1947: whether it would 'strike its own original path', setting its own goals, and finding appropriate solutions to its problems, or whether it would 'stumble in the wake of Europe', abandoning everything that made it unique in its effort to emulate Western methods. 'No doubt', Sri Aurobindo continued in his letter,

people talk of India developing on her own lines, but nobody seems to have very clear or sufficient ideas as to what those lines are to be. In this matter I have formed ideals and certain definite ideas of my own, in which at present very few are likely to follow me, since they are governed by an uncompromising spiritual idealism of an unconventional kind and would be unintelligible to many and an offence and stumbling-block to a great number. But I have not as yet any clear and full idea of the practical lines; I have no formed programme.[12]

The 'spiritual idealism' that Sri Aurobindo referred to was the vision of things that he had arrived at as a result of his yogic practices. This outlook did not exclude the life and actions of men, but it saw the outer in terms of the inner, based action on the realization of spiritual truth. Now that India was on the road to independence the most urgent need of its people was to become aware of their country's true spirit, and of its destined work in the world so that 'the future India may be indeed India'. Political self-determination remained the immediate goal, but the 'greater issue' (as he wrote a few months later) was whether independence would open the way to 'the beginning of a great Self-Determination not only in the external but in the spiritual' field as well.[13]

Eight months after rejecting Baptista's offer, Sri Aurobindo was invited by B. S. Moonje, current Chairman of the Reception Committee of the Indian National Congress, to preside over the 1920 Congress session. This request to accept the greatest honour that the national movement could bestow was not without political motivation. There is reason to believe that Sri Aurobindo was nominated at least partly because his retirement had placed him outside the current conflict between supporters and opponents of Gandhi's non-co-operation movement. Sri Aurobindo had little enthusiasm either for the policies of the old school, made up of his former Extremist associates, or for the new and somewhat faddish approach of Gandhi. This lack of involvement, he wrote Moonje, would make him an unsuitable president:

I am entirely in sympathy with all that is being done so far as its object is to secure liberty for India, but I should be unable to identify myself with the programme of any of the parties. The President of the Congress is really the mouthpiece of the Congress and to make from the presidential chair a purely personal pronouncement miles away from what the Congress is thinking and doing would be grotesquely out of place.

This and other purely political reasons were enough in themselves to keep Sri Aurobindo from accepting Moonje's offer. But the 'central reason' for his refusal, he wrote, was 'that I am no longer first and foremost a politician, but have definitely commenced another kind of work with a spiritual basis'. This, he informed his correspondent, he had taken up 'as my mission for the rest of my life'.[14]

Sri Aurobindo's 'work with a spiritual basis' will form the subject of Chapter 13. He did not begin to give it concrete form for several years, because he had resolved not to take up his 'practical work' until he had achieved *siddhi* or perfection in yoga. To do so, he wrote to his brother Barin in April 1920,* was 'not an easy thing'. But, he continued,

when the process is complete, there is not the least doubt that God through me will give this supramental perfection to others with less difficulty. Then my real work will begin. I am not impatient for the fulfilment of my work. What is to happen will happen in God's appointed time. I am not disposed to run like a madman and plunge into the field of action on the strength of my little ego. Even if my work were not fulfilled, I would not be disturbed. This work is not mine, it is God's. I listen to no one else's call.

Barin had asked Sri Aurobindo whether he would soon be coming to Bengal. Sri Aurobindo answered that, so far as he could see, his home province was not ready for what he had to give. But he added that for the moment he was staying where he was 'not because Bengal is not ready, but because I am not ready. If the unripe goes amid the unripe, what can he accomplish?'[15]

---

* Sentenced at Alipore to transportation for life, Barin was released in January 1920 as part of the amnesty declared on conclusion of the War.

CHAPTER NINE

Brahman and Vasudeva

In the preceding chapters we have dealt almost exclusively with Sri Aurobindo's external life. Occasionally we have looked at his intellectual development, and from time to time glanced at his spiritual growth; but for the most part we have been content to narrate outward events: birth, education, career, literary output, political activities. The deficiencies of this approach are obvious: it treats the three main aspects of his personality in reverse order of importance. For, when Sri Aurobindo's life is viewed in perspective, it is clear that his greatest and most characteristic achievements were in the spiritual field. His political and intellectual activities are best seen as he himself saw them: as expressions of his spiritual consciousness.

Still, it is hardly possible to avoid the outward approach to biography, because the documents upon which it must be based record external events. These materials provide an indispensable knowledge of the outer structure of a man's life. The emotions, the mind, and the spirit, essential to a full definition of personality, are more elusive. This is true even when the man's accomplishments are undistinguished. In proportion as he devotes himself to intellectual activities, the importance of his outer acts diminishes; and when his real spiritual life begins to unfold, they fade into relative insignificance. Some people, therefore, consider it impossible to write the life of a spiritual figure at all. Sri Aurobindo himself was of this opinion. What truly mattered in the life of a spiritual man, he wrote,

is not what he did or what he was outside to the view of the men of his time (that is what historicity or biography comes to, does it not?) but what he was and did within; it is only that that gives any value to his outer life at all. It is the inner life that gives to the outer any power it may have and the inner life of a spiritual man is something vast and full and, at least in the great figures, so crowded and teeming with significant things that no biographer or historian could ever hope to seize it all or tell it. Whatever is significant in the outward life is so because it is symbolical of what has been realized within himself and one may go on and say that the inner life also is only significant as an expression, a living representation of the movement of the Divinity behind it.[1]

If we applied these general observations to Sri Aurobindo's own life, we would be forced to conclude that a biography of him could give only a superficial picture of what he was. He affirmed that this was so. Asked to comment on a life-sketch that someone had sent him, he wrote: 'I see that you have persisted in giving a biography—is it really necessary or useful? The attempt is bound to be a failure, because neither you nor anyone else knows anything at all of my life; it has not been on the surface for men to see.'[2] Fortunately Sri Aurobindo provided his own solution to the problem that 'no biographer or historian could ever hope to seize' the truth of his inner life: he wrote about it himself. In autobiographical notes, in talks, in letters, and in a recently published diary, he provided a significant amount of information about his spiritual growth.

Still, in making a study of Sri Aurobindo's (or of anyone's) spiritual life, a biographer encounters special difficulties. To begin with, the very existence of the spirit has never been objectively established, and it is not generally admitted by the mind of the present century. If one accepts it as a postulate in order to inquire into its possible workings, two further difficulties emerge: the lack of hard data, and the lack of clear interpretive guidelines. Sri Aurobindo's accounts of his spiritual experiences are the only information on his inner development that we have or ever shall have. But these accounts are authentic, plentiful, and of diverse origin. Together they may constitute the richest documentation of the spiritual development of an advanced yogin that has ever been made available.

It is one thing to scrutinize descriptions of spiritual experiences, quite another to interpret them. Unlike such disciplines as history and literary criticism, the study of spirituality has no generally accepted hermeneutic framework. Spiritual experiences are not available on demand, nor do they lend themselves well to intellectual systematizing. We shall therefore not attempt a critical interpretation of Sri Aurobindo's spiritual life, but hope that our work of collation and commentary will serve a useful purpose.

We saw in Chapter 4 that Sri Aurobindo began to practice yoga around 1904. Even earlier, however, he had had a number of spontaneous spiritual experiences. These included 'a vast calm which descended upon him at the moment when he stepped first on Indian soil after his long absence' (1893), 'the vision of the Godhead surging up from within when in danger of a carriage accident in Baroda in the first year of his stay' (1893 or 1894), 'the realization of the vacant Infinite ... in Kashmir' (1903), and 'the living presence of Kali in a shrine on the banks of the Narmada' (around 1905).[3] These are all significant experiences but they did not immediately turn him to a life of spiritual seeking, for he had dedicated himself to his country's service. When he did take up yoga it was neither as a philosopher seeking an intellectual solution to the enigma of the universe nor as a religious man looking for an escape from the rounds of *karma* and rebirth, but rather as a man of action in search of strength and guidance to help him in his work. Not that Sri Aurobindo was without philosophical or spiritual interests. He had been attracted to Vedanta while still a student in England, and in Baroda he had begun to develop an original interpretation of the Upanishads and Gita. For centuries these scriptures had been looked on by most people as advocating inaction and renunciation. Shankaracharya, the chief exponent of the dominant school of Vedantic interpretation, the *mayavada* or doctrine of illusion, had declared: 'Brahman, the absolute reality, is true; the world is a lie.' The things of the world, and action in the world, had to be renounced to allow the individual self to be liberated in a state of union (yoga) with the Brahman. Sri Aurobindo at first accepted this interpretation; but, as his understanding of Vedanta grew more profound, he became convinced that Shankara's interpretation was not in perfect accord with the texts. The Upanishads and the Gita did *not* insist on the unreality of the world, nor did they demand inaction. The Isha Upanishad said clearly: 'doing verily works in the world', a man ought to live out his alloted span. The Gita said just as clearly: 'action is better than inaction'. Once Sri Aurobindo realized that life and works were not inconsistent with yoga, that, indeed, in the words of the Gita, yoga was 'skill in works', he felt free to begin sadhana.

He started with the breathing exercises known as pranayama. He continued this practice in Calcutta but the demands of public life made it impossible for him to be regular. Irregularity in pranayama can lead to dangerous disorders. In Sri Aurobindo's case it resulted in a serious illness that incapacitated him during the last months of 1906.[4] He did not fully recover until April the next year, and then found that he had lost his spiritual momentum. Through the whole of 1907 he suffered a 'complete arrest' of spiritual experience.[5]

Yoga is usually practised under the guidance of a guru. Sri Aurobindo had encountered a number of spiritual teachers but had received initiation from none of them. He had learned pranayama from a friend—a fact that helps explain his near-fatal illness. The friend's guru, Swami Brahmananda of Ganganath, had impressed Sri Aurobindo favourably; but he had never considered becoming Brahmananda's disciple.

While searching for a preceptor for his 'ashram' at Manicktolla, Barindrakumar Ghose had met several yogins. One, a Maratha named Vishnu Bhaskar Lele, had given him an opening to spiritual experience. Barin told Sri Aurobindo that Lele was the real thing. At this moment, the end of 1907, Sri Aurobindo was (as he later explained) 'groping for a way, doing no Sadhana at all, making no effort because I didn't know what effort to make, all having failed'.[6] Wishing to obtain guidance from a competent yogin, he agreed to Barin's suggestion to meet Lele.

After the Surat Congress Sri Aurobindo went to Baroda to see old friends, deliver speeches, and take a look at the state of the national movement in Gujarat. Barin wired Lele, then in Gwalior, to come to Baroda. The yogin arrived and met Sri Aurobindo at Khaserao Jadav's house. Sri Aurobindo explained that he was not interested in renunciation but wanted to practice yoga in order to obtain spiritual strength for his work. Lele replied, interestingly, that this would not be difficult for Sri Aurobindo since he was a poet.

Sri Aurobindo's fame as a nationalist leader was now at its height. Everyone in Baroda was clamouring to see him. Lele told him that the two of them would have to retire to a secluded place for a few days. Sri Aurobindo agreed and they went secretly to the *wada* of a friend in the heart of Baroda. What happened next is best told in Sri Aurobindo's own words:

'Sit in meditation,' he [Lele] said, 'but do not think, look only at your mind; you will see thoughts *coming into it*; before they can enter throw these away from your mind till your mind is capable of entire silence.' I had never heard before of thoughts coming visibly into the mind from outside, but I did not think either of questioning the truth or the possibility, I simply sat down and did it. In a moment my mind became silent as a windless air on a high mountain summit and then I saw one thought and then another coming in a concrete way from outside; I flung them away before they could enter and take hold of the brain and in three days I was free.[7]

In the 'concrete consciousness of stillness and silence' that had completely replaced his sense of self, there arose 'the awareness of some sole and supreme Reality'—what he would later identify as the 'passive Brahman'. This experience was 'attended at first by an overwhelming feeling and perception of the total unreality of the world'. By a strange irony, Sri Aurobindo had been engulfed by the very experience that is the basis of the mayavada philosophy that he had previously rejected:

There was no ego, no real world—only when one looked through the immobile senses, something perceived or bore upon its sheer silence a world of empty forms, materialised shadows without true substance. There was no One or many even, only just absolutely That, featureless, relationless, sheer, indescribable, unthinkable, absolute, yet supremely real and solely real.

Sri Aurobindo did not question or attempt to interfere with this experience. Indeed, he later wrote, there was no separate 'Sri Aurobindo' to question or interfere. He lived in the selfless awareness of the supreme Reality for days, for months, 'before it began to admit other things into itself' and 'realisation added itself to realisation'.

At an early stage the aspect of an illusionary world gave place to one in which illusion is only a small surface phenomenon with an immense Divine Reality behind it and a supreme Divine Reality above it and an intense Divine Reality in the heart of everything that had seemed at first only a cinematic shape or shadow. And this was no reimprisonment in the senses, no diminution or fall from supreme experience, it came rather as a constant heightening and widening of the Truth; it was the spirit that saw objects, not the senses, and the Peace, the Silence, the freedom in Infinity remained always, with the world or all worlds only as a continuous incident in the timeless eternity of the Divine.[8]

Mayavada was true, but not the sole truth. From his new state of consciousness Sri Aurobindo saw the beings and objects of the world not as the separate things they appear to us to be, nor as the empty names and forms (*nama-rupa*) of the Illusionists, but as real images or manifestations of the one Reality.

The series of experiences presented above have been related almost entirely in Sri Aurobindo's own words in order to avoid misrepresentation. They are experiences of a different order from those that men ordinarily have, and the possibility of verbal distortion is great. Even when great care is taken with the language, it is almost impossible to avoid apparent contradictions and paradoxes. To give one example, Sri Aurobindo said that when he entered the passive Brahman, the sense of self, of 'I', disappeared completely. And yet in describing the experience he used the first person pronoun. This is not the place to attempt to resolve such seeming discrepancies, or to enquire into the validity of spiritual experience.* The most pragmatic intelligence using the most scientific methods can neither prove nor disprove the existence of phenomena that, if they have any meaning at all, must lie beyond its scope. It will be more fruitful to mirror the attitude adopted by Sri Aurobindo when these experiences burst on his awareness, an attitude itself scientific in a manner appropriate to the subject: 'to accept' the self-validating reality that had impressed itself upon him 'as a strong and valid truth of experience, let it have its full play and produce its full experimental consequences'.[9]

In order to see more clearly what these truths and consequences were, it will be helpful to examine the experiences sequentially, as though they were quite separate from one another. There was, first, the complete silencing of the mind, followed by a perception of 'Something real but ineffable' that in positive terms could be described as 'some sole and supreme Reality', but which carried

---

* It is, however, a good place to define 'spiritual experience' and the related term 'spiritual realization', both of which occur frequently in this and later chapters. In letters written during the 1930s, Sri Aurobindo explained that 'experience is a word that covers almost all the happenings in yoga', i.e. becoming aware of the divine peace, presence, force, bliss, etc. Realization is when such experiences, instead of coming as 'flashes, snatches or rare visitations', become 'very positive or frequent or continuous or normal' and the thing realized becomes 'more real, dynamic, intimately present to the consciousness than any physical thing can be' (*Letters on Yoga* 877, 885, 879).

with it 'the negation of all that the mind can affirm as Being', a nirvana (literally, 'extinction') of the universe and of everything in it. What was seen was 'only a mass of cinematographic shapes unsubstantial and empty of reality'. The body continued to act, but only 'as an empty automatic machine'.[10]

This condition—the mental silence, the release from ego, the perception of an ineffable reality behind the vacant phenomena of the world—'remained unimpaired for several months'. But gradually 'the sense of unreality disappeared and there was a return to participation in the world-consciousness'. At the same time a new mode of action began: 'something else than himself took up his dynamic activity and spoke and acted through him but without any personal thought or initiative'.[11] This new dynamic power revealed itself dramatically when he was called on to resume his political work. Just before delivering a speech in Bombay, Sri Aurobindo told Lele that he had nothing to say: his mind was absorbed in utter silence. 'Lele told him to make *namaskara* to the audience and wait and speech would come to him from some other source than the mind.' And 'so, in fact, the speech came'.[12] It was one of Sri Aurobindo's most powerful public utterances:

You call yourselves Nationalists. What is Nationalism? Nationalism is not a mere political programme; Nationalism is a religion that has come from God; Nationalism is a creed which you shall have to live. Let no man dare to call himself a Nationalist if he does so merely with a sort of intellectual pride, thinking that he is more patriotic, thinking that he is something higher than those who do not call themselves by that name. If you are going to be a Nationalist . . . you must do it in the religious spirit. . . .

It is not by any mere political programme, not by National Education alone, not by Swadeshi alone, not by Boycott alone, that this country can be saved. . . . These are merely ways of working; they are merely particular concrete lines upon which the spirit of God is working in a Nation, but they are not in themselves the one thing needful. What is the one thing needful? . . . [It is to have] one over-mastering idea, one idea which nothing can shake, . . . the idea that there is a great Power at work to help India, and that we are doing what it bids us.[13]

The action that Sri Aurobindo carried out in this way was not limited to a single inspired address. The speech in question was in fact the sixth or seventh that he had delivered since his meeting with Lele; and during his return to Calcutta he delivered six or seven more. He had, in addition, to speak to innumerable people about politics and revolution (in Poona he was taken to a bomb factory and asked for his comments), not to mention having to engage in conversations with his hosts, with former students, and with enthusiastic admirers. All during this round of activity, 'the inner peace and freedom which resulted from this realisation [of the passive Brahman] remained permanently behind all surface movements and the essence of the realisation itself was not lost'.[14] In yogic terms Sri Aurobindo had achieved a 'status of an inner passivity and an outer action independent of each other': a simultaneous but separate realization of the passive and the active Brahman.[15]

Sri Aurobindo's resumption of action after having entered the silence of Brahman was, in our opinion, the principal turning-point in his life. A yogin who realizes Brahman has no need to proceed further. In the words of the Taittiriya Upanishad: 'The knower of Brahman reacheth that which is supreme.' Some might think that this experience, apparently devoid of warmth and colour, would hardly be worth having. But no one who has had it has ever thought so. Absolute knowledge brings absolute bliss. Commenting on the line just quoted from the Taittiriya, Sri Aurobindo wrote:

The knowledge of the Brahman is not a thing luminous but otiose, informing to the intellectual view of things but without consequence to the soul of the individual or his living. . . . The highest state of our being is not a denial, contradiction and annihilation of all that we now are; it is a supreme accomplishment of all things that our present existence means and aims at, but in their highest sense and in the eternal values. . . . The highest consciousness is integrally fulfilled in wideness and power of its existence, but also it is integrally fulfilled in delight. . . . Our highest state of being is indeed a becoming one with Brahman in his eternity and infinity, but it is also an association with him in delight of self-fulfilment. . . . Delight of being is the continent of all the fulfilled values of existence which we now seek after in the forms of desire. To know its conditions and possess it purely and perfectly is the infinite privilege of the eternal Wisdom.[16]

To those who attain this supreme knowledge and felicity, the things of the world have no more attraction in themselves. Absorbed in Brahman, their action can be reduced to the bare minimum necessary for the maintenance of the body, until at last the body drops away and the absorption in Brahman becomes complete. Many realized yogins have lived such a life of spiritual inactivity. This path was open to Sri Aurobindo. He did not take it.

Sri Aurobindo left Bombay for Calcutta at the end of January 1908. Before parting from Lele he asked him for guidance, at the same time informing him that a mantra had risen within him. Lele began giving detailed instructions, then stopped and asked Sri Aurobindo whether he could follow implicitly the inner guide (*antaryamin*) who had given him the mantra. Sri Aurobindo replied that he could. Lele then told him to surrender to the inner guide. If he was able to do this completely he would have no further need of a human guru. Sri Aurobindo accepted this advice. Henceforward surrender to the Divine became the principle of his life and yoga.

A few weeks after Sri Aurobindo returned to Calcutta, Lele came there at the invitation of Barindrakumar Ghose. The yogin met Sri Aurobindo and asked him how his sadhana was progressing. Was he still meditating morning and evening? Sri Aurobindo answered that he was not. He did not add that he now was in a state of constant meditation. Lele told him that the devil had caught hold of him. Sri Aurobindo said nothing, confident that it was the Divine and not the devil that he was following. This marked the end of his relationship with Lele; but he always remained grateful to the yogin for the 'important help' that he had given him, which helped him discover the foundations of his sadhana.[17]

Sri Aurobindo once wrote that the experience he had with Lele, that of the passive Brahman, was the first of 'the four great realisations on which his [Sri Aurobindo's] Yoga and his spiritual philosophy are founded'.[18] The second realization was achieved a few months later, in Alipore jail. Here, as we saw, Sri Aurobindo, after being placed in solitary confinement, passed through a period of inner turmoil. He was able to re-establish his equilibrium by taking refuge with the Divine within him. At that moment he was given a copy of the Gita. Reading it he was able 'not only to understand intellectually but to realise what Sri Krishna demanded of Arjuna and what He demands of those who aspire to do His work, . . . to renounce self-will and become a passive and faithful instrument in His hands'.[19] This realization soon enlarged itself into an all-encompassing awareness of the Divine, seen as Krishna in the form of Vasudeva, 'as all beings and all that is':

I looked at the jail that secluded me from men and it was no longer by its high walls that I was imprisoned; no, it was Vasudeva who surrounded me. I walked under the branches of the tree in front of my cell but it was not the tree, I knew it was Vasudeva, it was Sri Krishna whom I saw standing there and holding over me his shade. I looked at the bars of my cell, the very grating that did duty for a door and again I saw Vasudeva. It was Narayana who was guarding and standing sentry over me. Or I lay on the coarse blankets that were given me for a couch and felt the arms of Sri Krishna around me, the arms of my Friend and Lover. . . . I looked at the prisoners in the jail, the thieves, the murderers, the swindlers, and as I looked at them I saw Vasudeva, it was Narayana whom I found in these darkened souls and misused bodies. . . . [In the courtroom] I looked and it was not the Magistrate whom I saw, it was Vasudeva, it was Narayana who was sitting there on the bench. I looked at the Prosecuting Counsel and it was not the Counsel for the prosecution that I saw; it was Sri Krishna who sat there, it was my Lover and Friend who sat there and smiled.[20]

Along with this universal vision of the Divine came a widening of Sri Aurobindo's individual awareness into what he later called the 'cosmic consciousness'. When this became established in him, he said, he lost the sense of the world's unreality that had accompanied his Brahman-experience.[21]

Sri Aurobindo's sadhana went on with great intensity during the year of his imprisonment and during the nine months of action that followed. Entering the subliminal worlds that lie behind man's ordinary life, glimpsed only in dream or in so-called altered states of consciousness, he had many visions and inner experiences. More important for his future yogic development, during his meditations in jail he took the preliminary steps towards his third and fourth fundamental realizations. These, and the rest of his sadhana between 1910 and 1926, form the subject of the next chapter.

CHAPTER TEN

A Spiritual Adventure

Sri Aurobindo's two realizations of 1908—that of the passive Brahman and that of the cosmic consciousness—are often regarded as the final goal of yoga. To him, however, they were 'essential steps' towards further realizations. What traditional yogas consider to be the end was 'as it were, the beginning' of Sri Aurobindo's, 'that is to say, the point where its own characteristic realisations commence'.[1] In writing this Sri Aurobindo was not implying that the traditional yogas were defective. If Brahman, the Reality, has any validity at all, it must necessarily be flawless. It is, as Sri Aurobindo wrote in *Arya*:

the highest and this highest is the all; there is none beyond and there is none other than it. To know it is to know the highest and by knowing the highest to know all. For as it is the beginning and source of all things, so everything else is its consequence; as it is the support and constituent of all things, so the secret of everything else is explained by its secret; as it is the sum and end of all things, so everything else amounts to it and by throwing itself into it achieves the sense of its own existence.[2]

When one of his disciples belittled the traditional yogas Sri Aurobindo was quick to set him straight: 'As for the depreciation of the old yogas as something quite easy, unimportant and worthless and the depreciation of Buddha, Yajnavalkya and other great spiritual figures of the past, is it not evidently absurd on the face of it?' The realization of the self, the basis of the traditional yoga of knowledge, was, he wrote, 'as much the aim' of his yoga 'as of any other'.[3]

But self-realization was not the only aim of Sri Aurobindo's yoga. 'The object sought after', he wrote in a letter of 1935, was not 'an individual achievement of divine realisation for the sake of the individual, but something to be gained for the earth-consciousness'. In most of the traditional yogas, the self-realized individual departs 'out of world and life into Heaven or Nirvana'. Sri Aurobindo denied that this was the necessary issue of yogic practice. 'A distinct and central object of his yoga', he wrote, was 'a change of life and existence'. This would be achieved by 'bringing in' a new power of consciousness, which he called 'the supramental'. To reach this power and to make it 'active directly in earth-nature' he spent more than four decades 'hewing out a road' in uncharted regions. It was with this in mind that he declared: 'Our Yoga is not a retreading of old walks, but a spiritual adventure.'[4]

In order to understand the nature of this 'adventure' better, we must first form a clearer conception of yoga—what it is and how it is practised. The Sanskrit word 'yoga' means 'union'. It has become, as Sri Aurobindo wrote in *Arya*, the 'generic name' in India 'for the processes and the result of processes by which we transcend or shred off our present modes of being and rise to a new, a higher, a wider mode of consciousness which is not that of the ordinary animal and intellectual man'.[5] No word in any Western language signifies these processes or this result so well; but the things signified are not exclusively Indian. All systems of spiritual discipline (as distinct from systems of religious belief or codes of conduct) may be considered systems of yoga. All of them aim at the attainment of union with the One Reality that underlies the beings and objects of the world and gives them their significance. Men and women ordinarily are engrossed in the multiplicity of phenomena—this person, that object, this hope, that desire, that fear—and therefore cannot see the underlying Unity. All systems of yoga provide methods for regaining contact with this Unity, conceived either as an impersonal Absolute or a personal divinity. These methods invariably include a form of self-discipline; most of them also demand some measure of renunciation and self-restraint. It is this that makes spiritual practice unattractive to most men and women. One is asked to renounce the ordinary pleasures of existence—which, however transitory and finally unsatisfying, are at least real and seizable—and offered in their place an abstract Entity, or else an anthropomorphic god that might in the end (who knows?) turn out to be a fiction.

So viewed, yoga would seem to be either an abstruse philosophical pastime or a chase after a retreating will-o'-the-wisp. In any case it could hardly be considered a practical endeavour. But this is exactly what Sri Aurobindo said that it was:

If the truth of our being is an infinite unity in which alone there is perfect wideness, light, knowledge, power, bliss, and if all our subjection to darkness, ignorance, weakness, sorrow, limitation comes of our viewing existence as a clash of infinitely multiple separate existences, then obviously it is the most practical and concrete and utilitarian as well as the most lofty and philosophical wisdom to find a means by which we can get away from the error and learn to live in the truth.[6]

The orthodox systems of yoga practised in India, that is the systems based on the Vedic-Vedantic tradition (which Sri Aurobindo referred to as 'Vedantic yogas'), ask the aspirant to withdraw his attention from the 'clash of infinitely multiple separate existences' and to fix it on the 'infinite unity' behind them. Implicit in most of these paths (as generally practised) is the assumption that the world is an illusory appearance created by the power known as maya. Since the world is unreal, active participation in the life of the world is discouraged. To obtain the peace and bliss of heaven the Vedantic yogin turns his back on earth.

Sri Aurobindo's realization of the passive Brahman showed him the truth behind this ascetic approach to yoga; his subsequent realizations showed him its incompleteness. His first realization was indeed accompanied by a sense of the unreality of the universe, but this feeling was later replaced by an awareness of all things as real expressions of the divine Reality. No longer could he look on the world as the creation of an illusory maya. He saw it instead as the self-manifestation of the *shakti* or creative energy of the Supreme.

Alongside the Vedantic tradition of yoga there has existed in India for many centuries a form of knowledge and practice that gives special importance to shakti. This is the yoga of the tantras. These esoteric Sanskrit texts figure the divine energy as Shakti, the female consort of Shiva, who is the Absolute.* The primary aim of

---

* The male-female symbolism of the tantras is sometimes ritually enacted in practices that have given tantric yoga the alluring or pejorative label 'the yoga of sex'. Such practices are not, as is sometimes supposed, the whole of tantric yoga; nor are they performed by genuine *sadhakas* as means of ordinary sexual gratification.

tantric yoga is the same as that of the Vedantic paths: the attainment of union with the One Reality by means of liberation (*mukti*) from the world of phenomona. But the tantras hold up a second object as well: unattached *bhukti* or enjoyment of the phenomenal creation. Seeing the world as a manifestation of *shakti*, the tantric tradition affirms its value. It should not be rejected, but enjoyed as a creation of the divine.

Sri Aurobindo had little acquaintance with the scriptures of the tantra. His own early sadhana followed the lines laid down in the chief Vedantic scriptures: the Upanishads and the Gita. But as he progressed he found himself moving towards tantra's double object, and when he came to formulate his own path he wrote that it 'starts from the method of Vedanta to arrive at the aim of the Tantra'.[7] It was, he said, a synthetic or integral yoga. Drawing on the essence of all paths but bound down by none of their forms, it had as its central principle 'a self-surrender, a giving up of the human being into the being, consciousness, power, delight of the Divine'.[8] This meant, 'in psychological fact', a 'progressive surrender of the ego with its whole field and all its apparatus to the Beyond-ego with its vast and incalculable but always inevitable workings'—the workings of the 'higher nature', the shakti, on the 'lower nature' of man. Sri Aurobindo went on to distinguish three main features of the action of the higher on the lower nature. These neatly characterize his whole approach to yoga:

In the first place [the higher nature] does not act according to a fixed system and succession as in the specialised methods of Yoga, but with a sort of free, scattered and yet gradually intensive and purposeful working determined by the temperament of the individual in whom it operates. . . .

Secondly, the process, being integral, accepts our nature such as it stands organised by our past evolution and without rejecting anything essential compels all to undergo a divine change. . . .

Thirdly, the divine Power in us uses all life as the means of this integral Yoga.[9]

As he said elsewhere, 'All life is Yoga'. His own sadhana exemplified this dictum. It was not confined to a single line of experience but ranged freely through many provinces of the inner kingdom. It was not tied down to a single practice or set of practices but made use of life in all its variety.

As we saw in the last chapter, Sri Aurobindo's first major realizations left him with 'a status of an inner passivity and an outer action independent of each other'. This was, he later wrote, 'a state of entire spiritual freedom'; but there was still 'an evident absence of integrality', for there remained 'a cleft of consciousness between the passive and the active Brahman'.[10] This 'cleft' was closed some time later, when he had his third fundamental realization, 'that of the supreme Reality with the static and dynamic Brahman as its two aspects'.[11] It is not known for certain when he had this in its fullness; but he took the first steps towards it while still in Alipore jail (1908–9). Three years later he wrote that his 'subjective Sadhana' had 'received its final seal and something like its consummation by a prolonged realization and dwelling in Parabrahman' (the supreme Reality). What remained for him to do, he wrote, was a sadhana 'for life, practical knowledge and Shakti [power], not the essential knowledge or Shakti in itself which I have got already, but knowledge and Shakti established in the same physical self and directed to my work in life'.[12] Two of the special features of Sri Aurobindo's sadhana that have been discussed above—the central role of shakti and the importance given to life—are readily apparent in this passage. Present also is another feature which will be dealt with below—the inclusion of the body in the final fulfilment.

Between 1912 and 1920 Sri Aurobindo kept a detailed account of his sadhana in a series of diaries known collectively as *Record of Yoga*.[13] This document is noteworthy in at least three respects. To begin with, it provides a first-hand account of the day-to-day growth of the spiritual faculties of an advanced yogin. Most spiritual diaries record the thoughts, struggles, and preliminary experiences of novices. If we wish to know the daily thoughts and acts of spiritual masters, we must turn to diaries kept by disciples, such as *The Gospel of Sri Ramakrishna*. A few advanced practitioners have left first-person accounts, but most of these, for example the autobiography of St Teresa of Avila, were written retrospectively. Sri Aurobindo set down his experiences in *Record of Yoga* immediately after their occurrence, at times while they were still happening. This gives it a strong sense of immediacy.

The language of *Record of Yoga* is bare, unliterary, often couched in arcane terminology. This makes for difficult reading. Sri Aurobindo's businesslike entries provide little 'inspiration' or uplift. They also discourage what might be called spiritual romanticism. What the *Record* does provide is a down-to-earth account of a multitude of events, great and small, inner and outer, in the life of a dedicated researcher. Sri Aurobindo once wrote to a disciple, 'I think I can say that I have been testing day and night for years upon years' his spiritual knowledge and experience 'more scrupulously than any scientist his theory or his method on the physical plane.'[14] The *Record* bears this out in detail. It may be looked on as the laboratory notebook of an extended series of experiments in yoga.

The fact that the experiments did not always turn out well attests to the *Record*'s authenticity. People attracted to the spiritual life often believe that great saints and yogins are above all struggles and sufferings. Sri Aurobindo gave the lie to this notion, at least as regards his own sadhana, in a letter of 1936: 'You write as if I never had a doubt or any difficulty. I have had worse than any human mind can think of. It is not because I have ignored difficulties, but because I have seen them more clearly, experienced them on a larger scale than anyone living now or before me that, having faced and measured them, I am sure of the results of my work.'[15] Before the publication of the *Record* such statements had to be accepted on faith. But when one reads, under the date 24 June 1913:

The Vani [voice] that guides in the script is largely a tejasic [over-enthusiastic] vani—the old tejas [energy] that seeks to justify errors & to exaggerate the siddhi [state of perfection]. There have been clear false-hoods uttered. This record therefore ceases to have a real utility. . . . [16]

one becomes aware, even if the language leaves one puzzled, that surrender to the divine guidance does not guarantee a trouble-free existence. Looking to the positive side, when one reads in an entry written a few days later:

The final purification of the system from the physical touches of Ashanti [trouble] continues. In the morning there was only a rich and abundant rupadrishti [vision of forms], very bright in colours and numerous in forms and groups, mostly crude, in the prana akasha [ether of life]; this was under stimulus. In the afternoon the depression of the tejas [energy] parted and the Krishna Kali [personality of the divine] emerged with the Rudra personality of Krishna; the kamananda [delight in the physical body] more continuous & persistent while walking. . . . [17]

one may understand little, yet feel justified in believing that the experiences so scrupulously recorded were genuine.

Sri Aurobindo's yoga as chronicled in the *Record* had seven main parts, each of which consisted of four elements. He therefore referred to the whole system as *sapta chatushtaya*, the seven tetrads. The schema of this system, set forth in a series of Sanskrit mantras, was, he said, a 'programme' or 'map' of his entire sadhana. As such it provides an overview of his spiritual development during the early part of his stay in Pondicherry.

Sri Aurobindo's 'yoga of self-perfection' (as he called it elsewhere) had four 'constituent elements' or objects: *shuddhi* or purification, *mukti* or liberation, *bhukti* or beatitude, and *siddhi* or perfection.* [18] To him the essence of purification was the ordering of the 'mixed and confused' action of the various parts of man's nature. Each part had to be set to its proper working—the mind to thought, the life to unattached action and enjoyment, etc. Perfect purification brought about the loosening of the bondage of nature, in particular the bond of *ahankara* or ego. This liberation, mukti, led to perfection of the individual nature, siddhi, and enjoyment of the essential delight of being, bhukti. [19] These four elements or objects made up the *sansiddhi chatushtaya* or tetrad of complete perfection. A 'general chatushtaya', this one was 'the means, the sum and the completion of all the rest'. [20] There were two other general chatushtayas: the *brahma chatushtaya* or tetrad of the divine being, and the *karma chatushtaya* or tetrad of the divine action. Sri Aurobindo left no full descriptions of these, but in a letter of 1916 he sketched their outlines. After the preliminary sadhana became 'firmer and more complete', he wrote,

the system is more able to hold consistently and vividly the settled perception of the One [Brahman] in all things and beings, in all qualities, forces, happenings, in all this world consciousness and the play of its workings. That founds the Unity and upon it the deep satisfaction and growing rapture of the Unity. . . .

When the Unity has been well founded, the static half of our work is done, but the active half remains. It is then that in the One we must see the Master and His Power,—Krishna and Kali as I name them using the terms of our Indian religions. . . . When that has been done, then we may hope to found securely the play in us of his divine Knowledge governing the action of his divine Power. [21]

* These same four constitute the object of tantric yoga (*The Synthesis of Yoga* 38).

The three general chatushtayas delineated the goal of Sri Aurobindo's yoga. The means were put forward in the four chatushtayas of the instrumental nature. First came *samata chatushtaya*,
the tetrad of 'equality'. The basis of Sri Aurobindo's yoga, and the
'first necessity' for those wishing to practice it, was an invariable
inner equilibrium. For this four things were needed:

first equality in the most concrete practical sense of the word, *samata*,
freedom from mental, vital, physical preferences, an even acceptance of
all God's workings within and around him; secondly, a firm peace and
absence of all disturbance and trouble, *shanti*; thirdly, a positive inner
spiritual happiness and spiritual ease of the natural being which nothing
can lessen, *sukham*; fourthly, a clear joy and laughter of the soul
embracing life and existence [*atma prasada* or *hasyam*].[22]

It was not necessary, insisted Sri Aurobindo, to flee from the
world, or to reject its beings and objects, in order to develop this
equilibrium. The real task was to learn to bear 'the touches of
outward things' (the *bahya sparsha* of the Gita) without getting
disturbed, and eventually to take an equal delight (*sama ananda*)
in all things.

Next in order, though not necessarily in sequence (for all parts
of the yoga had to be worked on simultaneously) was *sakti
chatushtaya*, the perfection 'of the temperament or nature in the
lower system [consisting of] mind, life and body'. For this the
energy of the divine temperament (*virya*) had to be brought into
the human personality. At the same time the various parts of the
being had to be attuned to the peak condition of their power
(shakti). For this to be done perfectly, the divine nature, *daivi
prakriti*, had to be invoked, and its workings accepted with an
enlightened faith, *shraddha*.[23]

It was not enough to elevate the ordinary powers of the human
being to their highest level of working. Other powers, beyond the
range of man's normal functioning, had also to be cultivated.
Many people have had momentary experience of one or more of
these powers: intuitions, premonitory dreams, unexpected abilities. Modern Western researchers have made the study of such
'parapsychological phenomena' a legitimate, if not universally
respected, scientific discipline. In India, these powers, termed in
Sanskrit siddhis, have for centuries been studied, classified, and,
according to persistent tradition, deliberately used.

In Sri Aurobindo's sadhana, the siddhis formed part of the third or *vijnana chatushtaya*. Its four elements were *jnanam* or divine thought, *trikaladrishti* or direct knowledge of past, present and future, *ashta siddhi*, the eight psychical and physical siddhis, and *samadhi* or yogic trance. The *Record* shows that Sri Aurobindo had abundant experience of these extraordinary powers. But they were to him incidental to the central process of his sadhana: the change of his consciousness from a predominantly mental to a predominantly supramental power. He had made the discovery of 'the higher planes of consciousness leading to the Supermind' while still in Alipore jail. Later he began the process of 'ascent' into these planes, and of receiving the 'descent' of their powers into his consciousness. This discovery and this dual process constituted the fourth of the four fundamental realizations of his yoga.[24]

The terms 'plane', 'ascent' and 'descent' require elucidation. The physical universe may be seen as a 'general settled poise or world of relations ... between the Soul and nature'. There were, wrote Sri Aurobindo, other poises or worlds, which were 'practically, different harmonies from the harmony of the physical universe; they occupy, as the word "plane" suggests, a different level in the scale of being.'[25] He distinguished seven principal planes. The first three were those we are familiar with: matter, life, and mind. According to physical science, these are simply different forms of activity of physical substance. The Indian spiritual tradition, which Sri Aurobindo accepted, regards them as separate worlds, together making up the *aparardha* or lower hemisphere. The higher hemisphere (*parardha*) consists of pure existence, pure consciousness, and pure bliss (*sat-chit-ananda*), which together comprise the nature of the absolute Reality. According to Sri Aurobindo, between the upper and lower hemispheres there was a link-plane, which he called 'supermind'. This was not, as the name might suggest, a higher activity of mind. It was a different power altogether, as different from mind as mind is from life and life is from matter. Because he visualized the plane of supermind as lying 'above' mind, life and matter, Sri Aurobindo spoke of a movement of consciousness in its direction as an 'ascent' and referred to the inflow of energies from it as a 'descent'.

As Sri Aurobindo rose towards supermind, he became aware that between it and the lower levels there was an intermediate plane of 'supraconscient cosmic Mind', to which he gave the name 'overmind'. This plane, he said, was the ultimate source of man's higher intuitions, indeed it was the determining source 'of all movements below it and all mental energies'. As if with 'the wide wings of some creative Oversoul' it covered 'this whole lower hemisphere of Knowledge-Ignorance', serving as a link between mind-life-body and the Truth-consciousness of Supermind. At the same time, regarded from below, it took the form of a 'brilliant golden Lid' that veiled 'the face of the greater Truth from our sight, intervening with its flood of infinite possibilities as at once an obstacle and a passage in our seeking of the spiritual law of our existence, its highest aim, its secret Reality'.[26]

For many years Sri Aurobindo strove to overcome this 'obstacle' and negotiate this 'passage'—a delicate task, for, if the obstacle simply were done away with, the passage would disappear. The crucial process was the descent of the power or 'Godhead' (as he called it) of overmind into his physical being. It was announced that this had taken place on 24 November 1926, a day commemorated since as that of his siddhi or 'perfection'.

For most of us, to whom 'supermind' and 'overmind' are at best intellectual abstractions (though they were to Sri Aurobindo, he said, more concrete than anything apprehensible by the senses), it is difficult to understand the significance of their 'descent'. We have dealt with this process at some length because it was central to the 'change of life and existence', which, as we saw at the beginning of this chapter, Sri Aurobindo considered to mark the fundamental difference between his path and others. He wrote: 'There is a dynamic divine Truth (the supermind)' that 'into the present world of Ignorance . . . can descend, create a new Truth-Consciousness and divinise Life. The old yogas go straight from mind to the absolute Divine', bypassing the supermind and intermediate levels such as overmind. These yogas 'regard all dynamic existence as Ignorance, Illusion or Lila [play]; when you enter the static and immutable Divine Truth, they say, you pass out of cosmic existence.'[27] Sri Aurobindo, on the other hand, envisaged a transformation of cosmic existence by the power of supermind. In one of his last writings he gave a moving prognostication of this process:

As Nature has evolved beyond Matter and manifested Life, beyond Life and manifested Mind, so she must evolve beyond Mind and manifest a consciousness and power of our existence free from the imperfection and limitation of our mental existence, a supramental or truth-consciousness. . . .

Into that [spiritual] truth we shall be freed and it will transform mind and life and body. Light and bliss and beauty and a perfection of the spontaneous right action of all the being are there as native powers of the supramental truth-consciousness and these will in their very nature transform mind and life and body even here upon earth into a manifestation of the truth-conscious spirit.[28]

The physical side of this transformation—the remoulding of the body, 'even here upon earth' into a fit vehicle of the transformed consciousness—was the culminating object of Sri Aurobindo's yoga. It had as its base the four elements of the *sharira chatushtaya* or tetrad of the body: *arogya* or health, *utthapana* or lightness, *saundarya* or beauty, and *vividhananda* or varied physical delight. *Record of Yoga* contains many references to these four powers. It is a remarkable feature of Sri Aurobindo's yoga that the last two, beauty and bliss, were looked on not as tools of the devil but as legitimate, indeed indispensable elements of the total perfection.

Much of Sri Aurobindo's later practice of yoga was directed towards the effectuation of the physical transformation. He considered 'this part of the endeavour' to be 'the most difficult and doubtful',[29] and he did not look forward to full success in his lifetime. But he believed that whatever he accomplished would help in the eventual establishment of a divine life on earth, in a body, and not only in an unsubstantial heaven or nirvana.

Sri Aurobindo's sadhana after the 'overmental descent' is not well documented. This is unfortunate for it seems probable that after 1926 he went beyond the basic elements of the seven chatushtayas. One thing that can be gathered from scattered references in letters is that his spiritual occupations during the 1930s and 40s included an effort to bring the supramental light and power into overmind. In order better to accomplish this, he withdrew from outward contacts. In February 1927 he moved to a house adjoining the one he had lived in since 1922. Here, in a suite of three rooms on the first storey, he remained in solitude for the next twenty-four years. During this period his ashram took shape under the guidance of his spiritual collaborator, the Mother. From his seclusion he oversaw the development of this community of seekers, while continuing his own sadhana, and producing a great mass of prose and poetic literature.

CHAPTER ELEVEN

A Philosophy of Experience

A biography, particularly one as brief as this, is not the place for a lengthy analysis of the thought and writings of its subject. On the other hand, to ignore the intellectual life of a significant figure in the history of philosophy would be to err in the opposite direction. Sri Aurobindo's principal work in prose, *The Life Divine*, is regarded by some as one of the most important metaphysical treatises of the present century. Another book, *The Synthesis of Yoga*, presents the same philosophy from the point of view of yogic practice. These works were based largely on the Vedic-Vedantic tradition, but Sri Aurobindo's reading of the scriptures of this tradition was highly original. His expositions of the Gita and Upanishads strove to recover the original sense of Vedanta, and his interpretation of the Vedas has helped deliver those ancient texts from learned oblivion. Nor were Sri Aurobindo's intellectual interests confined to spiritual philosophy and scriptural exegesis. He made substantial contributions to social science, literary criticism, and Indian cultural history, and touched suggestively on such topics as linguistics and anthropology. His eight major prose works, and numerous shorter ones, were thus concerned with many different provinces of knowledge; yet they embodied a consistent outlook, expressing in intellectual language the vision of yoga. In this chapter we will examine the characteristics and development of Sri Aurobindo's thought, especially as exemplified by the philosophy of *The Life Divine*. The presentation of the central argument of that book, and the brief remarks on the themes of the others, are meant primarily as illustrations of the author's mode of thinking, and not as an exhaustive critique of his works.

In considering Sri Aurobindo as a philosopher and thinker we must begin with the paradox that this author of numerous volumes not only denied being a philosopher but even asserted that his works were produced without the aid of thought. 'And philosophy!' he once wrote to a disciple, 'Let me tell you in confidence that I never, never, never was a philosopher—although I have written philosophy which is another story altogether.'[1] To another disciple who beleaguered him with questions, he wrote: 'You expect me still to "think" and what is worse think what is right or wrong. I don't think, even; I see or I don't see.'[2] Both of these statements, as the contexts make clear, were made tongue in cheek. But both had serious intent. Sri Aurobindo was not speaking lightly when he explained that after his experience of Brahman in 1908 his mind remained always in a state of silence. 'From that moment, in principle,' he once wrote, 'the mental being in me became a free Intelligence, a universal Mind, not limited to the narrow circle of personal thought as a labourer in a thought factory, but a receiver of knowledge from all the hundred realms of being and free to choose what it willed in this vast sight-empire and thought-empire.' In that 'absolute silence of the mind' Sri Aurobindo 'edited the *Bande Mataram* for 4 months and wrote 6 volumes of the *Arya*, not to speak of all the letters and messages' he wrote after *Arya* ceased publication.[3]

That an impressively complete and coherent philosophy could be conceived (if that is the right word) and expressed without thinking is, to say the least, difficult for the mind to grasp. It is necessary at least to realize that Sri Aurobindo looked on philosophy not as an intellectual exercise but as the articulation of truths arrived at through inner experience. He had a deep-rooted distrust of intellectual systematizing indulged in for its own sake. In one of his earliest commentaries on the Upanishads he noted tartly, 'There is one great capacity of the learned and cultured mind both in Europe and Asia which one should admire without imitating; it is the capacity of dexterous juggling with words.'[4] A few years later he enlarged on the same theme: 'There is no human pursuit more barren and frivolous than metaphysics practised merely as an intellectual pastime, a play with words and thoughts, when there is no intention of fulfilling thought in life or of moulding our inner state and outer activity by the knowledge which we have intellectually accepted.'[5]

To mould one's 'inner state and outer activities by the knowledge' expressed in a philosophy of being is to practice yoga. The task of philosophy, according to Sri Aurobindo, was to formulate the relationship between 'the psychological and physical facts of existence' and 'any ultimate reality that may exist';[6] its purpose was to help the individual live and act in accordance with these facts, seen in terms of this reality.

Academic philosophers would accept this task but not this purpose. Some of them, therefore, would refuse to consider Sri Aurobindo's metaphysics as philosophy properly speaking. His writings, asserts one such critic, are deficient in the essential attributes of philosophy: logical argumentation and dialogue with other philosophers (as evidenced by quotations from their works).[7] If these attributes are accepted as final, it would have to be conceded that Sri Aurobindo wrote no philosophy. His books contain few mentions of past philosophers and no quotations from their works, and he avoided involved logical arguments:

There is very little argument in my philosophy [he once wrote]—the elaborate metaphysical reasoning full of abstract words with which the metaphysician tries to establish his conclusions is not there. What is there is a harmonising of the different parts of a many-sided knowledge so that all unites logically together. But it is not by force of logical argument that it is done, but by a clear vision of the relations and sequences of the Knowledge.

When he did use 'intellectual abstractions, ratiocination or dialectics', he wrote elsewhere, it was 'to explain my philosophy and justify it to the intellect of others'.[8] He did this very competently. Even the critic who wrote that Sri Aurobindo's lack of argument disqualified him as a philosopher placed him 'among the greatest speculative metaphysicians in human history'.[9]

Sri Aurobindo looked on metaphysics as a handmaid of life and action. In the midst of a profound discussion of the nature of the universe—was it an 'active objectivity' with no reality apart from the consciousness that observed it, or was it a self-existent material reality—he commented:

The difference, so metaphysical in appearance, is yet of the utmost practical import, for it determines the whole outlook of man upon life, the goal that he shall assign for his efforts and the field in which he shall circumscribe his energies. For it raises the question of the reality of cosmic existence and, more important still, the question of the value of human life.[10]

Thus he regarded the ancient controversy between Materialist and Idealist not as a stimulating intellectual debate but as a dialogue with practical applications. It would be possible indeed to regard *The Life Divine* as fundamentally a guide to life; but it is far from being a naive manual of conduct. Its complex view of existence embodies a theory of man that is concerned not only with his cognitive functions but also his will-to-power and will-to-delight. In the course of its fifty-six chapters it touches on many of the problems that have occupied philosophers since the time of Yajnavalkya and Thales, and provides original solutions to them.

Before examining this definitive statement of Sri Aurobindo's philosophy, we will look briefly at his development as a thinker. Academic critics usually attempt to trace the sources of their subject's work. This is a legitimate endeavour so long as it is based on real evidence and not mere speculation. Some writers have tried to demonstrate the influence of Greek and European philosophy on Sri Aurobindo. There is little positive evidence of such influence. He did read some of the Greeks at Cambridge, not as philosophers (philosophy was not part of his classical curriculum) but as masters of a genre of Greek literature. He found Aristotle 'exceedingly dry' but admired Plato, whose *Symposium* he used as a model for his *Harmony of Virtue*. Sri Aurobindo made no systematic study of European metaphysics either in England or later. He once went through a book on Hegel (who was much read at Cambridge in the 1890s), but it 'left no impression' on him. He put down Kant after struggling through a page or two and did not profit from reading a book on Bergson. The little he knew about European philosophy, he wrote, he 'picked up desultorily' in his 'general reading'. The Western thinkers he did respond to—Plato, Plotinus (with whom he had only a passing acquaintance) and Nietzsche—he admired not for their philosophical systems but for their inspired expression of intuitive ideas or inner experiences.[11]

In about 1903 Sri Aurobindo began reading the Upanishads and the Gita in Sanskrit. These became the basis of his 'first practice of Yoga' and, after his sadhana bore fruit, the first formative influence on his philosophy. 'I tried to realise what I read in my spiritual experience and succeeded', he later wrote; 'in fact I was never satisfied till experience came and it was on this experience that later on I founded my philosophy.'[12] It was the texts of the Upanishads and Gita (and later the Rig-veda) that he was interested in, not commentaries and secondary works. He did read epitomes such as the *Vedanta-sara*, and was familiar with the *bhashyas* of Shankara and others, but early on he made a distinction between the original Vedanta of the texts and the derivative philosophy of the commentators. His own commentaries, which he began to write at this time, gave evidence almost from the start of an unwillingness to rest content with accepted explanations that ran counter to his own intuitions.

As Sri Aurobindo's sadhana progressed his intuitions were replaced by what he referred to as 'direct Knowledge'. This revelation was the second of the two acknowledged sources of his philosophy. When he began to ascend into the planes between mind and supermind, he wrote, ideas 'came down in a mighty flood which swelled into a sea of direct Knowledge always translating itself into experience, or they were intuitions starting from an experience and leading to other intuitions and a corresponding experience'.[13]

Between his arrival in Pondicherry in 1910 and the launching of *Arya* in 1914, Sri Aurobindo presented the insights that came to him in this way in the form of commentaries on the Upanishads, particularly the Isha Upanishad, which he believed held the secret of 'The Life Divine'.* His initial intention was to bring out the original meaning of the texts: 'to rescue' them, as he put it, 'from the obscuration of quietistic philosophies'. But he also found it convenient to use the Vedanta of the Upanishads as a framework for his own developing philosophy. There were two reasons for this endorsement. First, he had, he said, experienced the central idea of Vedanta, the absolute Brahman, as an undeniable reality. Second, Vedanta, in his reading, had an attitude towards life that was as affirmative and dynamic as his own. It had a 'supreme utility', he wrote, 'for life, for man's individual and racial evolution'.[14]

Before long, however, Sri Aurobindo found that his inner experience seemed to surpass anything dealt with explicitly in the

* This phrase, later famous as the title of his principal philosophical treatise, was originally used as the title of the most extensive of these commentaries.

Upanishads. When this happened, he could no longer use his Upanishadic commentaries as a means of presentation of his own philosophy. He felt strongly that the only legitimate function of exegesis was to bring out the original sense of the text under study. Accordingly, when *Arya* began publication, he made a clear distinction between his interpretation of Vedanta and Veda, which he set forth in a number of translations and commentaries, and his own thought, which he elaborated in *The Life Divine*.

In the tongue-in-cheek letter cited in the beginning of this chapter, Sri Aurobindo related the story of the starting of *Arya*:

How I managed to do it [write philosophy] and why? First, because Richard proposed to me to co-operate in a philosophical review—and as my theory was that a Yogi ought to be able to turn his hand to anything, I could not very well refuse; and then he had to go to the war and left me in the lurch with sixty-four pages a month of philosophy all to write by my lonely self. Secondly, because I had only to write down in the terms of the intellect all that I had observed and come to know in practising Yoga daily and the philosophy was there automatically.[15]

The first part of this statement—that Sri Aurobindo wrote his major philosophical works only because Paul Richard decided to publish a magazine—was not, of course, intended to be taken literally. Before Richard settled in India, Sri Aurobindo had filled a dozen notebooks with philosophical writings and had planned more than one book on the subject. *Arya* provided him with a vehicle for the expression of a philosophy that already had taken form in his mind.

Sri Aurobindo's principal objection to philosophy as ordinarily written was that it achieved consistency and completeness only by isolating one aspect of truth from the rest. 'A philosophical system,' he wrote, 'is only a section of the Truth which the philosopher takes as a whole.'[16] When he came to formulate his own world-view he sought to avoid this error by taking an integral approach that derived from his own experience. Writing about the knowledge from the higher planes which was the second acknowledged source of his philosophy, he noted: 'This source was exceedingly catholic and many-sided and all sorts of ideas came in which might have belonged to conflicting philosophies but they were here reconciled in a large synthetic whole.'[17] This synthetic experience was reflected in a synthetic method. He proceeded not by isolation and analysis but by affirmation and a search for a higher harmony. This keynote was struck in the first chapter of *The Life Divine*: 'All problems of existence are essentially problems of harmony. They arise from the perception of an unsolved discord and the instinct of an undiscovered agreement or unity.'[18] The discords that Sri Aurobindo attempted to harmonize in *The Life Divine* included the great dualities whose opposition makes existence a puzzle and life an ordeal: Spirit and matter, God and the world, the personal and the impersonal, being and becoming, the one and the many, the individual and society, determination and free-will, action and silence, works and knowledge, renunciation and enjoyment. Regarding both members of each pair as valid, he reconciled them in a comprehensive synthesis. Thus, following the lines of his own experience, he affirmed the absolute reality of Brahman but did not deny the reality of the phenomenal world. Brahman was real, the world a real manifestation of its reality. This was the central pair of opposites, to whose reconciliation Sri Aurobindo devoted *The Life Divine*'s first book: 'Omnipresent Reality and the Universe'.

If the world is a manifestation of the divine perfection, why do we perceive it as a field of conflict, full of painful experiences or incomplete fulfilments that always fall short of perfection? Sri Aurobindo answered this question in the second book of *The Life Divine*, 'The Knowledge and the Ignorance—the Spiritual Evolution'. Brahman, the Omnipresent Reality, has 'involved' itself in its self-created opposite. In its own nature Brahman is Existence, Consciousness, and Bliss (*sat-chit-ananda*). Giving its consent to the mysterious urge of its creative energy to manifest even the negative possibilities inherent in its nature, it casts itself into non-being, unconsciousness, and insensibility. From this basis, termed by Sri Aurobindo 'the Inconscient', the creative energy reascends through the levels of matter, life, and mind until it reaches a 'supramental' level from which it can repossess *sat-chit-ananda*, and yet remain in contact with the three lower levels.

But why did the absolute and perfect Brahman have to involve itself in this apparently imperfect relative world, where the separate beings it has become must experience falsehood, pain, and evil? Sri Aurobindo answered that Brahman freely accepts imperfection 'only for one reason. for delight'. *Ananda*, the essential delight of being, is Brahman's 'eternal business', 'a harmony of various strains, not a sweet but monotonous melody [is] the message of his music'. Brahman accepts 'the lower notes also' in order to surcharge them 'with a deeper and finer significance'.[19] Put otherwise, Brahman descends into form for the 'delight of the adventure'. But this 'game' (*lila*) is not just for the fun of it, it 'carries within itself an object to be accomplished', namely 'a manifestation of the greater powers of Existence till the whole being itself is manifest in the material world in the terms of a higher, a spiritual creation'. This is 'the teleology of the evolution'.[20] Sri Aurobindo regarded evolution as fundamentally an unfolding of higher powers of consciousness, and only outwardly a development of more complex forms. Life emerges in matter because the principle of vitality is involved in matter. (The workings of DNA and related molecules would not, in Sri Aurobindo's view, 'explain' life. He saw the physical basis of inheritance as the mechanism of something irreducible to a form or activity of matter.) In life, increasingly complex structures are evolved, until a new principle, mind, is able to manifest, rudimentarily in the animal, more securely in man. (Sri Aurobindo scoffed at attempts to explain away consciousness as an epiphenomenon of the nervous system. The brain, he said, is the structure that allows consciousness to act in an organized way in living matter, but consciousness exists prior to its cerebral instrument.) Man looks on mind as the summit of creation. So, presumably, would a self-aware trilobite have regarded nervous life. According to Sri Aurobindo, however, mind is not the end product of evolution. Man is a 'transitional being'. Just as life emerged in the proto-bacterium, and conscious mentality in the proto-anthropoid, so supermind will emerge in the human prototype of a yet-to-be-evolved superior being, which Sri Aurobindo called 'the superman'. Since man is a conscious being, this evolutionary transition from man to superman will be a conscious process. Man can participate in his own self-exceeding. The name given to this participation is yoga, which is essentially an aspiration to the creative power behind evolution and a surrender to its workings.

In *The Life Divine* Sri Aurobindo gave considerable attention to the individual, whom he considered 'the key of the evolutionary movement'. But he was convinced that the aim of this movement was something more than individual fulfilment. The agent of the

supramental stages of evolution would be an individual not separate from and competing with other individuals, but one who,
aware of 'the Divine Reality in him which is also the Divine
Reality in others', would act 'for the Divine in others and the
Divine in all'. This 'gnostic individual' would thus find himself 'not
only in his own fulfilment, which is the fulfilment of the Divine
Being and Will in him, but in the fulfilment of others'. Many
gnostic individuals acting together would give rise to 'a new
common life superior to the present individual and common
existence'. Far from being 'void of vital savour', this 'evolution in
the Knowledge' would 'be a more beautiful and glorious manifestation' than the evolution in the Ignorance that we know. 'The
gnostic manifestation of life would be more full and fruitful and its
interest more vivid than the creative interest of the Ignorance; it
would be a greater and happier constant miracle'. Such a life, 'a
life of gnostic beings carrying the evolution to a higher supramental status might fitly be characterised as a divine life', Sri
Aurobindo wrote in the concluding chapter of his book, 'for it
would be a life in the Divine, a life of the beginnings of a spiritual
divine light and power and joy manifested in material Nature'.[21]

In this summary I have emphasized two features of the philosophy
of *The Life Divine* that are characteristic of all Sri Aurobindo's
thought: its synthetic method and its evolutionary resolution. Both
of these characteristics are found also in his other major works.
The very title of *The Synthesis of Yoga* shows that Sri Aurobindo's
aim in writing it was not to assert the superiority of one form of
yoga over another but to find the essential element in all of them
and use this to arrive at a harmony of their methods. Yoga has
traditionally been divided into three main 'paths': the yoga of
knowledge (*jnanayoga*), the yoga of devotion (*bhaktiyoga*), and
the yoga of works (*karmayoga*). There are also specialized paths
like *rajayoga*, *hathayoga*, and the various tantric disciplines. Each
path directs its attention to a different instrument: the mind, the
emotional being, the will, the 'inner instrument' of rajayoga, the
body, the subtle vessel of shakti. The aspirant is asked to concen-
trate exclusively on the workings of that instrument in order to
awaken its latent powers, and through them rise to union with the
Absolute. An undesirable side effect of this concentration is that
the aspirant often becomes incompetent in other parts of his

nature. The jnanayogin, for example, concentrating on the discriminative function of pure intellect, tends to become deficient in emotional responsiveness and active ability. If he is persistent, he achieves silence of mind, and through that the experience of Brahman; but at the same time his instrumental nature atrophies.

Sri Aurobindo's intention in the *Synthesis* was to show how all the paths of yoga could be harmonized in what he called an 'integral yoga'. In the first three parts of the book he surveyed the paths of works, knowledge, and devotion, pointing out their underlying similarities and indicating 'how they meet so that one starting from knowledge could realize Karma and Bhakti also and so with each path'. In the fourth part he turned to his own yoga of the seven chatushtayas, called here 'the yoga of self-perfection'. When this part was finished, he wrote in a letter of 1932, he intended 'to suggest a way in which all [paths] could be combined, but this was never written'.[22] When *Arya* ceased publication 'The Yoga of Self-Perfection' was only a third finished. Some years later Sri Aurobindo revised the first part of the book, but unfortunately he never completed his planned synthesis.

In *The Human Cycle* and *The Ideal of Human Unity* Sri Aurobindo gave special attention to one of his recurrent themes: the significance of man's collective existence, and the right relation of the individual man to the collectivity. Although he spoke little of yoga in these books, they may be looked on as attempts to apply the unifying vision of yoga to sociology and history. In *The Human Cycle*, originally called *The Psychology of Social Development*, he showed that human societies, like human individuals, pass through certain 'psychological' stages on their way to a pre-ordained evolutionary fulfilment. Using terms borrowed from the German historian Karl Lamprecht, he called these the symbolic, typal, conventional, individual, and subjective stages. Then, going beyond Lamprecht, he envisaged 'the coming of a spiritual age' of human society. Sri Aurobindo characterized the first three stages as 'infrarational'. With the emergence of the self-aware individual came the development of reason, and the questioning of the assumptions that had given stability to the infrarational order. The establishment of a new order awaits the emergence of a 'suprarational' power, for reason has shown itself incapable of resolving the conflicting demands of opposed individuals, groups, and nations. The way to harmony is through the development of subjectivity, but not the false subjectivity that equates the self with the individual ego. There must be an effort to find the universal self that is one in all. When a critical mass of self-realized individuals comes together, 'a spiritualised society' will take form which will 'live like its spiritual individuals, not in the ego, but in the spirit, not as the collective ego, but as the collective soul'.[23]

The Human Cycle treats the problem of the individual and society from an inner, psychological point of view. *The Ideal of Human Unity* studies the same general theme from a more outward, political standpoint. In the course of this study of ancient and modern history Sri Aurobindo showed that political entities evolved according to a predictable pattern. Isolated units were brought together in pre-national empires (like the Roman). These eventually broke apart into segments that became the basis of separate nation-states. At a certain stage in their development the stronger nation-states attempted to build national empires (like the British); but such groupings lacked the internal consistency necessary for long survival. By the early twentieth century another trend had become apparent: an attempt to arrive at a voluntary world-union in which 'the religion of humanity' would replace the various creeds and ideologies that had hitherto divided mankind. Sri Aurobindo foresaw that a dangerous obstacle to the emergence of a world-union would be the growth of a totalitarian world-state. The rise of Nazi Germany and Stalinist Russia justified his apprehensions. A true world union could never be achieved by forcing a uniform outlook on the constituent units. The correct balance would be found in a 'unity in diversity', each group expressing its own character while participating in the common life of the whole.

In *The Future Poetry* Sri Aurobindo demonstrated that even literature exhibited an evolutionary movement, passing through stages characterized by different sources of inspiration. He used the course of English poetry to illustrate this thesis. First there was a stage, exemplified by Chaucer, in which English poetry was chiefly concerned with the depiction of the physical life. The next stage, typified by the Elizabethans, celebrated the life of the heart and will, the play of the emotions and the trials of passion. There followed an era of predominantly intellectual verse, noble in Milton, petty in Dryden and Pope. The so-called romantic period was, in Sri Aurobindo's view, the first glow of the dawn of a higher, more spiritual inspiration. Blake, Wordsworth, and

Shelley brought this new element into English literature but they failed to establish it there. The Victorians fell back to a mental inspiration and expression, prettified with a few romantic touches. The most significant trend in early-twentieth-century poetry, as Sri Aurobindo saw it, was a renewed attempt, most evident in Yeats and A. E. (George William Russell), to give expression to a spiritual inspiration. The post-War literary revolution belied his hopes that a higher sort of poetry might soon develop in England. Modern verse, with its repudiation of regular rhythm, was, he thought, an inadequate vessel for the mantra-like movement that characterized true spiritual poetry, which so far had found full expression only in the Vedas and Upanishads.

CHAPTER TWELVE

Poet of Yoga

Sri Aurobindo's first published volume was a collection of poetry; his last book, on which he worked for more than three decades, was an epic poem. Between the issuing of *Songs to Myrtilla* in 1898 and the partly posthumous publication of *Savitri*, he brought out nine volumes of verse and left unpublished enough for several more. This large body of poetry has never achieved the popularity of his prose writings, but he himself gave it special value for two reasons. First, he was by predilection a poet rather than a philosopher. Second, he considered poetry superior to prose as a means of expression of spiritual experience. The truths that the mystic discovers are in their nature ineffable; finite words cannot convey the infinite. But poetry, by making fuller use of the subtler resources of language, is better able to communicate the mystic's 'intimations of immortality' than the more precise, less suggestive idiom of prose. In *The Future Poetry* Sri Aurobindo worked out a literary theory based upon this premise; in his poems he put his theory into practice.

Sri Aurobindo wrote in all the four major poetic forms: lyric, dramatic, narrative, and epic. In the present chapter we will briefly survey his production in each. My remarks are intended to highlight his growth as a poet and should not be taken as evaluative pronouncements. The quotations will help the reader form his own preliminary judgement.

Sri Aurobindo's early lyric verse is conventional both in form and in subject matter. The poems in *Songs to Myrtilla*, most of which were written in England, deal with love, patriotism, nature, sorrow, and death. All are rhymed, all arranged in familiar stanzas or couplets. The poems that he wrote in Baroda five to ten years later treat the same themes in verse that is at least outwardly of the same make. But the new poems show a great increase in evocative power. 'Night by the Sea', the most reflective poem in *Songs to Myrtilla*, has a few affecting passages:

> Love, a moment drop thy hands;
> Night within my soul expands. . . .
> Darkness brightens; silvering flee
> Pomps of foam the driven sea.[1]

A similar scene elicited a similar mood a decade later in 'The Sea at Night'; but the verse now is filled with palpable imagery and resonances:

> The grey sea creeps half-visible, half-hushed,
> And grasps with its innumerable hands
> These silent walls. I see beyond a rough
> Glimmering infinity, I feel the wash
> And hear the sibilation of the waves
> That whisper to each other as they push
> To shoreward side by side,—long lines and dim
> Of movement flecked with quivering spots of foam,
> The quiet welter of a shifting world.[2]

Some of the poems written in Baroda contain hints of Sri Aurobindo's turn towards the spiritual, of his 'longing . . . for new and lovelier things'.[3] Three or four of them even deal with frankly spiritual subjects. Here are three stanzas from 'Rebirth':

> Not soon is God's delight in us completed,
>   Nor with one life we end;
> Termlessly in us are our spirits seated
>   And termless joy intend.
>
> Our souls and heaven are of an equal stature
>   And have a dateless birth;
> The unending seed, the infinite mould of Nature,
>   They were not made on earth,
>
> Nor to the earth do they bequeath their ashes,
>   But in themselves they last.
> An endless future brims beneath thy lashes,
>   Child of an endless past.[4]

Religious poetry in English has a tendency to drift towards

prosaic sermonizing: witness Milton, Smart, even, for the most part, Donne and the other Metaphysicals. True spiritual poetry, as in Blake's lyrics, the early Wordsworth, the best of Shelley, does not necessarily, or even usually, use devotional or theological language to treat lofty themes. Sri Aurobindo knew this well, but in some of his later Baroda verse he came close to spiritual philosophizing. 'In the Moonlight' begins lyrically enough:

> If now must pause the bullocks' jingling tune,
>> Here let it be beneath the dreaming trees
>> Supine and huge that hang upon the breeze,
> Here in the wide eye of the silent moon.

But when the poet's reflections lead him to disturbing questions, his music begins to falter:

> Why is it all, the labour and the din,
>> And wherefore do we plague our souls and vex
>> Our bodies or with doubts our days perplex?
> Death levels soon the virtue with the sin.

The poem then becomes an examination of the conflicting claims of science and spirituality. The resolution, as might be expected of Sri Aurobindo, is satisfyingly synthetic:

> [Man] rises to the good with Titan wings:
>> And this the reason of his high unease,
>> Because he came from the infinities
> To build immortally with mortal things;

> The body with increasing soul to fill,
>> Extend Heaven's claim upon the toiling earth
>> And climb from death to a diviner birth
> Grasped and supported by immortal Will.[5]

James Cousins, a minor figure in the Irish literary renaissance, who for some time lived in India, cited 'In the Moonlight' as exemplifying both the strengths and the weaknesses of Sri Aurobindo's poetry. The first stanzas, wrote Cousins, were 'superlative'; but much of the rest he considered 'poor minted coin of the brain'.[6] Sri Aurobindo did not agree with Cousins's strictures but he did find his criticism of 'great use' in moving 'towards a supra-intellectual style'.[7]

To understand what he meant by this we must familiarize ourselves with some of the ideas he developed in his critical writings. Poetry, he said, could be graded in two different ways, according to the source of its inspiration, and according to the degree of its rhythmic and verbal perfection. He felt that inspiration could come from any 'plane': physical, vital, psychic, mental, or those levels above the mind that he called 'overhead' planes. Poetry from each of these sources might be expressed with varying degrees of perfection: adequately, effectively, or in an illumined, inspired, or 'inevitable' way.* Illumined poetry of a vital inspiration (that is, expressive of the life-energy), such as one finds often in Shakespeare, was superior in poetic quality to adequate or less-than-adequate mental poetry, or even to poetry that dealt with spiritual things in an ordinary way. The very highest poetry came 'from the Overmind inspiration or from some very high plane of Intuition' and had 'the power to convey not merely the mental, vital or physical contents or indications or values of the thing uttered, but its significance and figure in some fundamental and original consciousness which is behind all these and greater'.[8] Sri Aurobindo called this supreme poetry 'the mantra', because he felt that the most perfect examples of it in world literature were the mantras of the Vedas. His own attempt to develop a supra-intellectual style was a conscious effort to bring the power of the mantra into English poetry.

Sri Aurobindo wrote few lyrics during his early years in Pondicherry. When he returned to the form in the 1930s he used it for the expression of his spiritual knowledge and experience. Here is his poetic evocation of 'Nirvana':

> All is abolished but the mute Alone.
> > The mind from thought released, the heart from grief
> > Grow inexistent now beyond belief;
> There is no I, no Nature, known-unknown.
> The city, a shadow picture without tone,
> > Floats, quivers unreal; forms without relief
> > Flow, a cinema's vacant shapes; like a reef
> Foundering in shoreless gulfs the world is done.

---

* Sri Aurobindo's categories give precision to Matthew Arnold's endeavour (in 'The Study of Poetry', an essay published while Sri Aurobindo was in England) to discover 'what poetry belongs to the class of the truly excellent'. Arnold declined to define the characteristics of 'the very highest poetical quality', preferring to give examples. Three of the passages he cited from classical and European literatures were also used by Sri Aurobindo to illustrate his theories.

> Only the illimitable Permanent
> Is here. A Peace stupendous, featureless, still,
> Replaces all,—what once was I, in It
> A silent unnamed emptiness content
> Either to fade in the Unknowable
> Or thrill with the luminous seas of the Infinite.[9]

This may be compared with the prose descriptions of the same experience that were quoted in Chapter 9. In the poem, suggestive imagery ('forms without relief/ Flow, a cinema's vacant shapes') combines with fittingly bare statement ('Only the illimitable Permanent/ Is here') to produce an impression more living and illuminating than that of the more sharply defined prose.

Almost all of Sri Aurobindo's lyric poetry was written in traditional forms. He believed that form was of 'supreme importance' in the search 'for poetic perfection'. In particular he affirmed that metre was 'not only the traditional, but also surely the right physical basis for the poetic movement'.[10] Most of his own poetry was written in familiar English metres and arranged in standard stanzas. 'Nirvana' demonstrates how even so conventional a form as the Petrarachan sonnet could be used to express a very uncommon experience. In some of his later lyrics he experimented with classical quantitative metres. The sapphics used in 'Descent' give the poem a rushing movement appropriate to the subject:

> All my cells thrill swept by a surge of splendour,
> Soul and body stir with a mighty rapture,
> Light and still more light like an ocean billows
>   Over me, round me.
>
> Rigid, stone-like, fixed like a hill or statue,
> Vast my body feels and upbears the world's weight;
> Dire the large descent of the Godhead enters
>   Limbs that are mortal.[11]

In 'Ocean Oneness' delicate alcaics are the musical framework of a metaphorical image:

> Silence is round me, wideness ineffable;
> White birds on the ocean diving and wandering;
> A soundless sea on a voiceless heaven,
>   Azure on azure, is mutely gazing.[12]

Sri Aurobindo felt that free verse cut itself off from most of the aural resources exploited by metrical poetry. His own attempts to find a balance between free movement and measured rhythm are of considerable interest but compare unfavourably with his metrical successes:

> Vast and immobile, formless and marvellous,
> Higher than Heaven, wider than the universe,
> In a pure glory of being,
> In a bright stillness of self-seeing,
> Communing with a boundlessness voiceless and intimate,
> Make thy knowledge too high for thought, thy joy too deep for
> emotion;
> At rest in the unchanging Light, mute with the wordless self-vision,
> Spirit, pass out of thyself; Soul, escape from the clutch of Nature.
> All thou hast seen cast from thee, O Witness.[13]

Most of the lyrics that Sri Aurobindo wrote in Pondicherry treat explicitly spiritual themes; but he did not believe that spiritual inspiration had to be confined to 'elevated' subjects. His own dramatic poetry illustrates this well. Between 1906 and 1916 he wrote five complete verse plays and drafts of two others. His description of the first one to be published, 'a romantic story of human temperament and life-impulses on the Elizabethan model',[14] applies to the others as well. The plays are 'romantic' both in the literary and the popular sense: each deals with 'events and characters remote from ordinary life'; and in each the protagonists are a strong handsome youth and a beautiful resourceful girl who fall in love and (except in the tragedy *Rodogune*) eventually get married. Like Elizabethan dramas, Sri Aurobindo's are based on diverse literary sources (Greek myth, *The Arabian Nights*, the *Kathasaritsagara*); are written in unrhymed iambic pentameter, with passages of prose; and are divided into five acts. In *The Future Poetry* Sri Aurobindo commented on the hold that Shakespeare has had over later English poets, causing some of the best of them to turn out second-rate verse-dramas: Wordsworth's *Borderers*, Shelley's *Cenci*, etc. He felt that the main error of these poets was their unthinking acceptance of the Elizabethan notion of 'drama as a robust presentation of life and incident and passion'. It was not necessarily wrong for them to have adopted the Elizabethan dramatic form, for 'after due modification' it might 'still be used for certain purposes, especially for a deeper life-thought expressing itself through the strong colours of a romantic interpretation'.[15] His own plays evidently were an attempt to introduce this 'deeper life-thought' into English dramatic verse. The difficulties of such an experiment are obvious; for drama, by its very nature, is bound down to outward speech and incident.

Some of the dialogue of *Perseus the Deliverer* could only have been written by a poet having considerable yogic knowledge. In the play the villain Polydaon is possessed by a supernatural entity who gives him temporary powers but ultimately destroys him. It was something of this sort, said Sri Aurobindo, that happened to Hitler and, on a lesser scale, to some of his own disciples. Perseus explains what occurs in such cases in a notable speech:

> This man for a few hours became the vessel
> Of an occult and formidable Force
> And through his form it did fierce terrible things
> Unhuman. . . .
> Then the Power withdrew from him
> Leaving the broken incapable instrument,
> And all its might was split from his body. Better
> To be a common man mid common men
> And live an unaspiring mortal life
> Than call into oneself a Titan strength
> Too dire and mighty for its human frame.[16]

Sri Aurobindo's other 'dramatic romances' (as he called them)—*The Viziers of Bassora*, *Eric*, and *Vasavadutta*—contain no overt expression of occult or yogic knowledge; yet all of them were written while he was deeply involved in yoga. He made three drafts of *Vasavadutta* in 1915 and 1916, a period when his sadhana was quite advanced and, incidentally, when he was writing sixty-four pages of philosophy every month. Why did he spend so much time retelling (delightfully enough) the love-story of Udayan and Vasavadutta? Would he not have been better employed writing a tract on *brahmacharya* for the use of his disciples? As we shall see in the next chapter, Sri Aurobindo's ideas about what constituted the yogic life were not determined by tradition or convention. One whose maxim was 'All life is yoga' might legitimately include human passion in his literary purview.

Like his plays, Sri Aurobindo's narrative poems are chiefly concerned with human love, but they regard it as a fall from more strenuous concerns. In 'Urvasie', Pururavus's longing for the beautiful *apsara* causes him to abandon his duties as king of Aryavarta. 'Driven by a termless wide desire', he wanders 'over snow and countries vague' until he reaches the abode of Lakshmi in the high Himalaya. The goddess, knowing what he seeks, addresses him:

> ...since thy love is singly great,
> Doubtless thou shalt possess thy whole desire.
> Yet hast thou maimed the future and discrowned
> The Aryan people...
> Their power by excess of beauty falls,—
> Thy sin, Pururavus—of beauty and love:
> And this the land divine to impure grasp
> Yields of barbarians from the outer shores.[17]

This poetic explanation of India's fall to foreign invaders was written just before the author took up the seemingly hopeless task of preparing his country for revolution. Biographical readings of imaginative literature are always risky; but it would not be far-fetched to regard 'Urvasie' as at least partly a poetic working out of two opposed impulses: the search for beauty and delight, and the urge to act forcefully in the world. A similar conflict is at the centre of 'Love and Death', written in 1899. This narrative, briefer and poetically superior to 'Urvasie', is based on the episode of Ruru and Pramadvara in the Mahabharata. In the poem, as in the Sanskrit epic, Ruru must give half his life to Yama to redeem his beloved Priyumvada (as Sri Aurobindo calls her) from death. Adding incident to the original bare story, Sri Aurobindo has his Ruru descend to Patala to make the required sacrifice. The boy's passage is through the depths of the ocean:

> He down the gulfs where the loud waves collapsed
> Descending, saw with floating hair arise
> The daughters of the sea in pale green light,
> A million mystic breasts suddenly bare,
> And came beneath the flood and stunned beheld
> A mute stupendous march of waters race
> To reach some viewless pit beneath the world.

Gladly Ruru gives half his span of life in exchange for Priyumvada; but first he is made to see what he is forfeiting—not, as Pururavus, earthly empire, but spiritual greatness:

> There Ruru saw himself divine with age,
> A Rishi to whom infinity is close,
> Rejoicing in some green song-haunted glade
> Or boundless mountain-top where most we feel
> Wideness, not by small happy things disturbed.
>   ...above this earth's half-day he saw
> Amazed the dawn of that mysterious Face
> And all the universe in beauty merge.

Yet Ruru does not regret his decision. 'Old essential earth' is dearer to him than the promise of heavenly bliss, and dearer still the body of his beloved:

> Thrilling he felt beneath his bosom her;
> Oh, warm and breathing were those rescued limbs
> Against the greenness, vivid, palpable, white,
> With great black hair and real and her cheek's
> Old softness and her mouth a dewy rose.[18]

Written five years before Sri Aurobindo took up yoga, 'Love and Death' foreshadows an important aspect of his philosophical and spiritual outlook: the inclusion of life and the physical existence in man's ultimate fulfilment.

After completing 'Love and Death', Sri Aurobindo thought about adapting a number of Mahabharata episodes in English verse; but he wrote only a canto or two of one such poem, 'Uloupi', a narrative based on the Arjuna-Ulupi story. When he returned to narrative poetry a few years later, his increasing political commitment induced him to take as his subject an incident from Indian history: the heroic stand of Baji Prabhu Deshpande, one of Shivaji's lieutenants, against a vastly superior force of Mughals. The opening of this poem, often quoted, is deservedly admired for its descriptive power:

> A noon of Deccan with its tyrant glare
> Oppressed the earth; the hills stood deep in haze,
> And sweltering athirst the fields glared up
> Longing for water in the courses parched
> Of streams long dead. Nature and man alike,
> Imprisoned by a bronze and brilliant sky,
> Sought an escape from that wide trance of heat.[19]

The longer Sri Aurobindo remained in India, the more he used indigenous material in his poetry; but he never repudiated his 'early cult for the work of the great builders' of Western literature.[20] In 1909, while imprisoned in Alipore jail, he began work on an epic that derived both form and theme from classical Greece. Since his school days he had looked on Homer's dactylic hexameter as perhaps the most perfect metrical instrument ever devised. He took interest in the efforts of poets like Longfellow and Clough to write in English hexameters; but he considered their attempts unsuccessful. *Ilion*, the epic he started in jail, was on the technical side an attempt to solve the problem of the hexameter in English. But it may be read simply as a poetic recreation of the last day of the Trojan war. The sun is a recurrent symbol in Sri Aurobindo's poetry. As 'Baji Prabhou' begins with a description of noon, so *Ilion* begins with an evocation of dawn:

Dawn in her journey eternal compelling the labour of mortals,
Dawn the beginner of things with the night for their rest or their ending,
Pallid and bright-lipped arrived from the mists and the chill of the Euxine.
Earth in the dawn-fire delivered from starry and shadowy vastness
Woke to the wonder of life and its passion and sorrow and beauty,
All on her bosom sustaining, the patient compassionate Mother. . . .[21]

Sri Aurobindo worked on *Ilion* steadily between 1910 and 1913, and afterwards revised the eight chapters that he had completed. But in 1915 he began another epic that would occupy him for the remaining thirty-five years of his life. The subject of the new poem was the story of Savitri and Satyavan. Early versions of *Savitri* are similar to 'Love and Death' and 'Uloupi' in form and in treatment. In all three poems a story from the Mahabharata is presented in unrhymed iambic pentameter verse. The Savitri story has some superficial similarity to the Ruru-Pramadvara episode, and it appears that Sri Aurobindo intended first to make *Savitri* another straightforward tale of love conquering death. But as he revised and re-revised his poem, he brought out more and more of the story's symbolic possibilities. Eventually *Savitri* became a poetic chronicle of his yoga, of equal importance in the corpus of his works to *The Life Divine* or *The Synthesis of Yoga*. It was, moreover, not merely a record of his sadhana, but a part of it. 'I used *Savitri* as a means of ascension', he wrote in a letter of 1936. 'In fact *Savitri* has not been regarded by me as a poem to be written and finished, but as a field of experimentation to see how far poetry could be written from one's own yogic consciousness and how that could be made creative.'[22] In other words the composition of *Savitri* was an endeavour to come in contact with the 'overhead planes' that are the native home of the mantra, and to give body to the knowledge and vision of those planes in revelatory speech.

In its final form, published in two volumes in 1950 and (posthumously) in 1951, *Savitri* extends to almost 24,000 lines. In Sri Aurobindo's telling of the story the girl Savitri, granted as a boon to the childless sage Aswapathy, is regarded as an incarnation of the Divine Mother. Aswapathy is a yogin aspiring 'for a universal realisation and a new creation'.[23] His upward quest is a metaphor for the process of 'ascent' in yoga. Sri Aurobindo's poetical description of the realms through which Aswapathy must pass constitutes his most detailed account of the geography of the inner worlds. But he did not create *Savitri* simply as a chart for the use of future explorers. He meant it as a rhythmical embodiment of his experiences that could awaken sympathetic vibrations in those who read it.

Savitri begins, like *Ilion*, with a description of dawn; but this 'symbol dawn', as Sri Aurobindo called it, clearly is something more than the diurnal return of the sun:

> It was the hour before the Gods awake.
> Across the path of the divine Event
> The huge foreboding mind of Night, alone
> In her unlit temple of eternity,
> Lay stretched immobile upon Silence' marge....
> An unshaped consciousness desired light
> And a blank prescience yearned towards distant change.
> As if a childlike finger laid on a cheek
> Reminded of the endless need in things
> The heedless Mother of the universe,
> An infant longing clutched the sombre Vast.
> Insensibly somewhere a breach began:
> A long lone line of hesitating hue
> Like a vague smile tempting a desert heart
> Troubled the far rim of life's obscure sleep....
> The darkness failed and slipped like a falling cloak
> From the reclining body of a god.
> Then through the pallid rift that seemed at first
> Hardly enough for a trickle from the suns,
> Outpoured the revelation and the flame.[24]

It will not be possible in this study adequately to discuss the poetic
qualities of *Savitri*, or even to reproduce a sufficient number of
extracts to exhibit its diversity and scope. The best way to conclude
the chapter will be to quote, without comment, a representative
passage:

> A marvellous sun looked down from ecstasy's skies
> On worlds of deathless bliss, perfection's home,
> Magical unfoldings of the Eternal's smile
> Capturing his secret heart-beats of delight.
> God's everlasting day surrounded her,
> Domains appeared of sempiternal light
> Invading all Nature with the Absolute's joy.
> Her body quivered with eternity's touch,
> Her soul stood close to the founts of the infinite.
> Infinity's finite fronts she lived in, new
> For ever to an everlasting sight. . . .
> There lightning-filled with glory and with flame,
> Melting in waves of sympathy and sight,
> Smitten like a lyre that throbs to others' bliss,
> Drawn by the cords of ecstasies unknown,
> Her human nature faint with heaven's delight,
> She beheld the clasp to earth denied and bore
> The imperishable eyes of veilless love.[25]

CHAPTER THIRTEEN

A Laboratory Experiment

Sri Aurobindo's life after 1920 had little outward incident. A narrator of documented events is left with almost none to relate. In 1926, after six years when he wrote practically nothing and progressively decreased his contacts with others, he withdrew into almost complete seclusion. Eventually he resumed his writing, but for twenty-four years he was virtually inaccessible except to a handful of associates. Even in retirement, however, he took an active interest in practical matters. Although his concentration on sadhana kept him from embarking personally on the 'outer work' that he long had planned, he presided over the transformation of his household into a diversified spiritual community that he considered a first step towards the greater society he envisaged.

As we have seen, Sri Aurobindo regarded yoga not as an escape from life but as a means of transforming it. Liberation made possible a selfless participation in the work of the world. During his stay in Alipore jail he received what he termed an *adesh* or 'command' to engage in a fourfold labour. Though he never spoke openly about this vocation he did, in a letter of August 1912, give an early disciple an outline of his programme. First there was a literary work, which he conceived at the time as a reinterpretation of the Indian tradition 'in all its parts, from a new standpoint'. Secondly, on the basis of this knowledge, he would establish a new method of yoga 'which will not only liberate the soul but prepare a perfect humanity'. Thirdly, since India was the intended centre of this work, it had to be restored to its 'proper place in the world'. Finally, 'a perfect humanity being intended', society would have 'to be remodeled so as to be fit to contain that perfection'.[1]

Up to 1910 Sri Aurobindo had given most of his attention to the third item on this list. For more than a decade he had worked for India's freedom, making use of both political and revolutionary methods. In Pondicherry he continued to support the national movement, but he became convinced that the right way to achieve freedom was 'by means of Yoga applied to human means and instruments, not otherwise'.[2] After 1910 his focus shifted from political to literary work. This he brought to an at least temporary state of completion in the seven volumes of *Arya* (1914–21). At the same time he was tracing out the path of his new method of sadhana, logging it for his own use in *Record of Yoga* and making it accessible to others in the *Synthesis*.

Thus by 1920 Sri Aurobindo had accomplished much under three of the four heads of his programme. Only the 'social' side of his work was undeveloped. He had made a start in this direction by encouraging Motilal Roy, the young man of Chandernagore who had harboured him there in 1910, to start a *sangha* or commune. At one time Sri Aurobindo thought of making this small group the nucleus of the larger community he hoped to establish when he returned to British India. But around 1921, after guiding Motilal's sangha for a number of years, he severed his connection with it when Motilal went his own way. But Sri Aurobindo did not abandon his plan of setting up 'centres' that would serve as training-grounds for his 'associates' in the 'large external work proceeding from the spiritual basis of this Yoga' to which he felt called.[3] One such centre was established in Bhawanipur, Calcutta, under the direction of his brother Barindrakumar. After observing its generally unsatisfactory development for a year or two, Sri Aurobindo asked Barin to close it in 1925. Attempts to set up a centre in Gujarat were even less successful. Eventually he concluded that a community of the kind he wanted only could prosper under his direct supervision.

By this time Sri Aurobindo had begun to think of his household in Pondicherry as a 'centre'; but it had not been founded as one. In its origin it was a practical arrangement necessitated by his life in exile. The young men who stayed with him and looked after his personal needs regarded him as an elder brother and friend, not as a guru. He wrote and did sadhana in his 'quiet unobtrusive way', giving them absolute freedom to do whatever they wished. Some of them took up sadhana of themselves, but others, Moni for instance, evinced no interest in yoga at all, and Sri Aurobindo (in the words of a contemporary diarist) '*never even once* told him anything about it'. He did, however, put silent inner pressure on all the members of his 'little colony', which he referred to in his letter of August 1912 as 'a sort of seed plot, a laboratory' for experiments in yogic living.[4]

In 1920 this inchoate community began to take more definite form. Two letters that Sri Aurobindo wrote during the year (both of which were cited, in another context, at the end of Chapter 8) give evidence of his increasing involvement in the 'social' aspects of his work. In April, he wrote to Barindrakumar Ghose about the *deva-sangha* or 'divine community' he hoped to found. Sri Aurobindo described this mostly in negative terms. By deva-sangha he did *not* mean a religious institution of the traditional variety. It would be, he wrote,

not a fixed and rigid form like that of the old Aryan society, not a stagnant backwater, but a free form that can spread itself out like the sea with its multitudinous waves—engulfing this, inundating that, absorbing all—and as this continues, a spiritual community will be established.

The community he envisaged would not exist in a rarefied spiritual atmosphere cut off from the creative activities of life:

Our business is not with the formless Spirit only; we have to direct life as well. Without shape and form, life has no effective movement. . . . We do not want to exclude any of the world's activities. Politics, trade, social organization, poetry, art, literature—all will remain. But all will be given a new life, a new form.[5]

This letter of April 1920 contains no indication that Sri Aurobindo had begun to put his ideas into practice. But in his letter to B. S. Moonje, written just four months later, Sri Aurobindo wrote that he had 'definitely commenced . . . a work of spiritual, social, cultural and economic reconstruction of an almost revolutionary kind', adding that he was 'even making or at least supervising a sort of practical or laboratory experiment in that sense which needs all the attention and energy that I can have to spare.'[6]

Note the repetition, after eight years, of the word 'laboratory'. The image is an appropriate one for a yogin whose approach to sadhana, as evidenced by the *Record*, was essentially scientific. Note also the sudden intensification of the 'experiment'. For more than ten years it had shown hardly any development; now it was demanding his full attention. Using hindsight, one can identify the catalyst of this change as Mirra Richard, who returned to Pondicherry with her husband Paul on 24 April 1920. Paul Richard, the French writer who had helped Sri Aurobindo launch *Arya* in 1914, was full of new plans and projects. Mirra was content to sit at the feet of Sri Aurobindo, whom she had inwardly accepted as her spiritual master. In December Paul Richard went on a tour of northern India, where he stayed for more than a year. Later he went back to Europe. Mirra remained with Sri Aurobindo. At this time there was only a handful of people gathered around him; but now their numbers 'showed a tendency to increase rather rapidly'.[7] Sri Aurobindo attributed this development to Mirra's dynamic nature, which he came to regard as the complement of his own. In a letter of 1926 he wrote that his personal force, representing the 'Purusha element', acted principally in the realm of spiritual knowledge, while Mirra's, 'representing the Shakti element' was 'predominantly practical in its nature'.*[8] In this letter Sri Aurobindo referred to Mirra as 'Mira Devi'. Soon afterwards he began calling her 'the Mother', a name that since Vedic times has been used for the creative shakti. Without the Mother, he said, his conception of a divine life on earth could never have been embodied.

Between 1920 and 1926 the number of Sri Aurobindo's disciples— now an appropriate term to describe them—grew from half a dozen to more than twenty. Arrangements had to be made for the newcomers' board and lodging. In 1922 Sri Aurobindo and the Mother moved to a new house on Rue de la Marine. The old place on Rue François Martin was kept for the accommodation of disciples and visitors. Later other houses in the neighbourhood were rented or bought. Around the time that *Arya* ceased publication Sri Aurobindo began issuing some of the shorter series from the journal as booklets; but this venture did not bring in sufficient money to support a growing community. The wherewithal for the expansion came mostly from admirers in Bombay, Gujarat, Bengal, and other places. Communal activities and services

---

* This characterization makes use of the Indian idea of existence as a male-female duality. Purusha, 'person', is the name given in the Sankhya philosophy to the masculine element, the conscious being. Shakti, 'power', is the name used in the Tantras for the feminine element, the executive force.

evolved as the need arose. Food for most of the disciples was prepared and served in Sri Aurobindo's house. In the rear was a small kitchen garden that was looked after by Barindrakumar Ghose. Woman disciples made and mended clothing. Torn *dhotis* were transformed into blouses that even the Mother wore.

The Mother took an active interest in the practical affairs of the community, but before 1926 she remained largely in the background. The life of the disciples revolved around A. G., as Sri Aurobindo was known. His unassuming ways surprised newcomers with traditional notions about how a *guru* should act. Those who wanted his *darshan* had to be satisfied with sitting near him as he read the morning paper. When he wished to send a telegram, he would offer the completed form to a group of disciples and say, with a hint of apology in his voice, 'I suppose this will have to be sent.' The disciples, far from feeling inconvenienced, would compete for the privilege of running the errand. Sri Aurobindo's feeling at the time was that the traditional *guru-shishya* relationship had lost much of its potency by becoming conventionalized. 'I have no confidence in guruhood of the usual type', he wrote in his 1920 letter to Barin. 'I do not want to be a guru. What I want is for someone, awakened by my touch or by that of another, to manifest from within his sleeping divinity and to realize the divine life.'[9]

Recognizably 'spiritual' activities grew up gradually during the twenties. Collective meditations began around 1922. They often were followed by an informal hour of talk, during which the disciples engaged Sri Aurobindo in discussions on a wide range of topics: Indian politics, world affairs, local events, books, medicine, education, literature, art—and also sadhana. His voice 'was soft and gentle, almost feminine', reports one who was present. On occasion he could be sharp, saying, with a quick gesture, 'Don't talk nonsense!'; but for the most part he spoke 'in a relaxed and jovial mood', often using humour to lighten serious subjects. Once, asked what would be the nature of the perfection resulting from the supramentalization of the physical being, he replied, with a comical wave of his hands, 'I have *no* idea.' When the laughter subsided, he went on: 'It is yet to be done. All I can say is that it would be something which would have in it the two fundamental laws of the supermind, truth and harmony.' A few moments later, questioned about the *siddhi* (power) of invulnerability, he replied,

'The best thing is when you have got the *siddhi* to get someone to beat you to find out whether you have become invulnerable or not.'[10]

Serious topics often called for more serious treatment. The following excerpt is from a talk of 1926:

The one thing sadhana has done for me is that it has removed all isms from my mind. . . .

What we are doing at present is making ourselves fit instruments of the higher truth, so that when it comes down there will be the proper instrumentation for its working. We won't reject life; we have to bring a new consciousness into the external work. . . .

Life has no isms in it, supermind also has no isms. It is the mind that introduces all isms and creates confusion. That is the difference between a man who lives and a thinker who can't. A leader who thinks too much and is busy with ideas, trying all the time to fit the realities of life to his ideas, hardly succeeds. While the leader who is destined to succeed does not bother his head about ideas. . . .

So far as I am concerned I have got my work and I am satisfied with it. Not that I have no idea about the work that will be done when the truth comes down. But immediately at present we have to bring down a change in the physical mind, the nervous being, and the vital mind, so that they may become fit instruments of the truth. That is a big enough work, I should think.[11]

Sri Aurobindo and the Mother did not expect the disciples to help actively in this work. The novices were in fact a great drain on their energy, and without them they certainly would have been able to advance more quickly. Why then did they accept disciples? Would it not have been better for the two of them to withdraw temporarily from outward contacts and to do intensive sadhana together in order to prepare a solid foundation for the 'external work'? When they began their collaboration, this possibility presented itself as one of two alternatives. The other was to let the disciples form themselves into a sort of prototype of the proposed divine community. The latter alternative prevailed, but not as a result of 'a mental choice', the Mother explained later. 'It came spontaneously. The circumstances were such that there was no choice; that is, quite naturally, spontaneously, the group was formed in such a way that it became an imperative necessity.'[12]

The community of *sadhaks* was required as a field of experimentation. If the force that Sri Aurobindo and the Mother were 'bringing down' was to extend itself into the environment, as they intended, they needed to know in detail how it acted on ordinary men and women. The only way to obtain such knowledge was to stock their 'laboratory' with voluntary guinea pigs and to see what happened when the force came down. If the metaphor seems brutal, it should be remembered that scores, later hundreds of prospective disciples were turned away, and that those who were accepted considered themselves extremely fortunate. Close to the objects of their devotion, able to surrender responsibility of their sadhana to them, many of the chosen ones made rapid progress.

Others, however, did not. Up to this point, the methods of yoga that Sri Aurobindo had given those who approached him were the methods that he himself had used. He advised aspirants to establish mental silence in order to experience the passive Brahman, to surrender to the dynamism of the active Brahman, to open to the inner guidance, and to try to see the Divine in all things and beings. Some disciples had preliminary realizations; but others got stuck or went astray. Much preparation is needed before an aspirant can safely ascend into the higher planes. Those who attempt to do so prematurely can get sidetracked into a dangerous 'intermediate zone' between the ordinary and the illumined consciousness and there lose balance or even go insane. And when the disciples descended into the subconscious and unconscious parts of their nature, as all who follow Sri Aurobindo's yoga must do, they tended to succumb to the darkness and inertia of those levels. Sri Aurobindo and the Mother went forward, sometimes rapidly, sometimes slowly; but many of the disciples floundered in place.

Realizing that most sadhaks would have difficulty following the path that he himself had taken, Sri Aurobindo began in the twenties to reformulate his sadhana in terms appropriate to neophytes. He introduced nothing completely new, but changed the focus in two important respects: in regard to the soul or 'psychic being' and in regard to the Mother. In the *Arya* he had placed special emphasis on the role played by the mind in sadhana. 'Man is a mental and not yet a supramental being', he wrote in the *Synthesis*. 'It is by the mind therefore that he has to aim at knowledge and realise his being.'[13] This emphasis was in accord with his own nature and experiences. It was through the silent mind that he had realized Brahman, through the higher levels of mind that he was approaching supermind. But Sri Aurobindo was aware that the ordinary mind has built-in limitations. Its characteristic operation is analysis: division and arrangement. But truth is a unity that can only be grasped by a synthetic vision. The analytic mind is 'incapable of knowing the supreme Truth; it can only range about seeking for Truth, and catching fragmentary representations of it, not the thing itself, and trying to piece them together'.[14] The levels of mind above the ordinary intellect, known to us as the sources of intuition and genius, do not have these inherent limitations; but it is not easy to establish a reliable contact with them. Many so-called intuitions are really the results of ordinary, sometimes rather tortuous reasoning, or even disguised subrational impulses. Sri Aurobindo cautioned beginners against uncritically following guidance that claimed to be intuitive. Instead, he advised them to follow the promptings of their soul. Since the word 'soul' is used rather vaguely in English for a number of different things, he preferred to employ another term he had borrowed from the Mother: 'psychic being'. From about 1926 he began to lay stress in his talks and letters on a process that he called the 'emergence' or 'coming forward' of the psychic being. It was this that his disciples should aspire for, for when the psychic came forward, all the rest would become safe and easy. 'When the psychic being comes in front,' he wrote in a letter, 'there is an automatic perception of the true and untrue, the divine and the undivine, the spiritual right and wrong of things, and the false vital [i.e., of the life-force] and mental movements and attacks are immediately exposed and fall away and can do nothing.'[15] Eventually the entire being would become transformed in the mould of the psychic. Then the more difficult, and dangerous, spiritual and supramental transformations could proceed more smoothly.

The second change of focus concerned the role of what Sri Aurobindo called the 'divine force' or force of the Mother. The principle of his yoga, he explained, was for the sadhak to open himself to the influence of this force: to aspire for its intervention, to reject everything that acted against it, and finally to surrender to its workings. To do this sincerely was, he said, not an easy task. One had to offer oneself completely, without making any personal demands. At the same time, one had to be vigilant that the force that one opened to was the real divine force, and not a disguised movement of the ordinary nature, or even an undivine or 'hostile' force.

Many readers, even those who admit the possibility of an inactive Absolute or disinterested Creator, may have difficulty accepting the existence of a conscious 'divine' or 'spiritual' force. But if there is any truth at all to spiritual development, there must be a spiritual force that produces spiritual results. Since ancient times aspirants in India and in other places have accepted the existence of such a force, and regarded it as having more than human potency. They rarely conceived of it in the impersonal terms used above. Rather they have worshipped it as a divinity: the Great Goddess, the Shakti, the Divine Mother. As we have seen, Sri Aurobindo looked on Mira, the Mother, as 'representing the Shakti element'. From around 1926, he began to encourage his disciples to approach her in this way. Since her 'spiritual knowledge' was 'predominatingly practical in its nature', it was she who best could guide them through the day-to-day difficulties of yoga.

In November 1926, after Sri Aurobindo had the 'overmental descent' described in Chapter 10, he ceased to meet his disciples. Henceforth, he told them, the Mother would look after their development. After his retirement the community of sadhaks, who now numbered some two dozen, began to be known as Sri Aurobindo's ashram. So far he had shunned this term because it had, like 'guru', acquired connotations he wanted to avoid. In Vedic times, ashrams were hubs of both spiritual and secular activity. But after the triumph of the world-denying philosophies they began to be looked on as places of retreat. Sri Aurobindo had no intention of letting his household turn into a monastery or hermitage. 'My aim', he wrote in a letter, 'is to create a centre of spiritual life which shall serve as a means of bringing down the higher consciousness and making it a power not merely for "salvation" but for a divine life upon earth'. He called the germ of this centre an ashram 'for want of a better word, for it is not an Ashram of Sannyasins, but of those who want to leave all else and prepare for this rule'.[16]

During the years of Sri Aurobindo's retirement the Mother came forward as the active director of the ashram's inner and outer life. The disciples came to her for guidance in work—she was a born organizer under whose direction the ashram's activities expanded in every direction—and also for help in sadhana and in life. They saw Sri Aurobindo only three times a year, when he gave darshan; but they were still able to communicate with him, at first through the Mother and later by means of letters. They sent him reports on their work and also daily records of their yoga- and life-experiences. For more than five years he attended to enormous masses of this correspondence, devoting as much as ten hours a day to it. Stern when necessary, but generally mild and even indulgent, he answered queries and gave encouragement and advice, addressing each of his correspondents in accordance with his or her nature. This meant replying to village women in simple Bengali, and engaging in intellectual thrust and parry with university graduates. Only rarely did he lay down the law. Faced with a specific spiritual or domestic problem he usually provided a specific solution, but he also offered guidelines that would help the disciple solve future problems on his own.

Sri Aurobindo's more significant replies were later collected and published in *Letters on Yoga*, a three-volume work that constitutes the most complete presentation of his yoga as given to others. It is remarkable, however, that nowhere in the two thousand pages of his published correspondence did he put forward a set method of practice. The 'perfect technique' for a yoga that aimed not only at personal liberation, but also at a transformation of the nature of the individual and eventually of the world, was not, he wrote, 'one that takes a man by a little bit of him somewhere, attaches a hook, and pulls him up by a pulley into Nirvana or Paradise. The technique of a world-changing yoga has to be as multiform, sinuous, patient, all-including as the world itself.'[17] This did not mean that experiences such as liberation in the Brahman consciousness were excluded from his yoga. The Brahman-experience had been the first step in his own sadhana, and it was a necessary stage for those who aspired to follow him. But most aspirants could achieve this and other fundamental experiences only after their minds, lives, and bodies had been prepared by a prolonged period of self-discipline. Most of Sri Aurobindo's letters on yoga deal with this preparatory stage.

Sri Aurobindo's ashram continued to grow even after his retirement in 1926. The number of disciples rose to 85 by the end of 1928, and to 150 a few years later. This seems to have been as many as Sri Aurobindo and the Mother then wanted.*[18] He considered attempts of disciples inside and outside the ashram to proselytize on his behalf 'a great difficulty'. He once wrote, in a humourous vein,

I don't believe in advertisement except for books etc., and in propaganda except for politics and patent medicines. But for serious work it is a poison. It means either a stunt or a boom—and stunts and booms exhaust the thing they carry on their crest and leave it lifeless and broken high and dry on the shores of nowhere—or it means a movement. A movement in the case of a work like mine means the founding of a school or a sect or some other damned nonsense. It means that hundreds or thousands of useless people join in and corrupt the work or reduce it to a pompous farce from which the Truth that was coming down recedes into secrecy and silence. It is what has happened to the 'religions' and is the reason of their failure.[19]

Sri Aurobindo had nothing against religion per se. He felt that each of the great religions had given something of value to the world. But he was convinced that no religion could transform humanity. 'A way to be opened that is still blocked, not a religion to be founded, is my conception of the matter,' he wrote.[20]

---

* The number of ashram inmates rose steadily from 85 in 1930 to 150 in 1934. There was no significant increase until 1938, when 172 inmates were counted. The next recorded count was 350 in 1942. The sudden jump was due to an influx from war-threatened Bengal.

CHAPTER FOURTEEN

Last Years

On the eve of the darshan ceremony of 24 November 1938, Sri Aurobindo stumbled while walking in his room, fell, and fractured his right thigh. It was a serious injury—an impacted fracture of the right femur above the knee—which required delicate handling. The leg was put in a plaster cast and gentle traction applied. In January the cast was removed and a course of physical therapy commenced; but it was more than a year before his activities were nearly as full as they had been before the accident. During his convalescence a team of disciples, most of whom had medical backgrounds, looked after his needs. These attendants stayed on even after his recovery was complete. His twelve-year period of complete seclusion was over.

Two weeks after the accident Sri Aurobindo began holding daily conversations with his attendants. These talks went on regularly until the end of 1940, and continued sporadically for several years more. As in the evening talks of 1923–6, Sri Aurobindo moved freely over a wide range of topics, alternating between, or combining, humour and seriousness. He could make the most difficult yogic realizations seem living and accessible, as this exchange shows:

Dr. Manilal: How can one succeed in meditation?
Sri Aurobindo: By quietude of mind. There is not only the Infinite in itself, but also an infinite sea of peace, joy, light, power above the head. The golden lid, *hiranmaya patra*,* intervenes between the mind and what

---

* A phrase from the Isha Upanishad. Elsewhere Sri Aurobindo spoke of the 'golden lid of overmind' in connection with this and another passage from the Upanishads (*Letters on Yoga* 103).

is above the mind. Once you break this lid [*making a movement of the hand above the head*] they [peace, joy etc.] can come down any time at your will. But for that, quietude is essential. Of course there are people who can get them without first establishing the quietude, but it is very difficult. . . .

Dr. Manilal: At one time I felt as if my head were lying at the Mother's feet. What does that mean, sir?

Sri Aurobindo: It is the experience of the psychic being. So you had the psychic experience.

Dr. Manilal: But unfortunately I couldn't recognise it. [*laughter*]

Sri Aurobindo: It is this 'I' that comes in the way. One must forget it, as if the experiences were happening to somebody else. If one could do this, it would be a great conquest. When I had the experience of nirvana [*in 1908*], I forgot myself completely. I was a sort of nobody. What's the use of Dr. Manilal So-and-so living with this 'I'? If in discovering your inner being, you even had died, it would have been a glorious death.

Dr. Manilal: What happens when the human consciousness is replaced by the divine consciousness?

Sri Aurobindo: One feels a perpetual calm, perpetual strength, one is aware of infinity and lives not only in infinity but also in eternity. One feels immortality and does not care about the death of the body. And then one has the consciousness of the One in all. Everything becomes the manifestation of the Brahman. For instance, as I look round this room, I see everything as the Brahman. No, it is not mere thinking. It is a concrete experience. Even the wall, the books are Brahman. I see you no more as Dr. Manilal but as the Divine living in the Divine. It is a wonderful experience.[1]

Sri Aurobindo's attendants often tried to get him to speak about himself, and they succeeded more than previous inquirers. Their records of his reminiscences are among the most important sources of his biography.

Sri Aurobindo's extended period of recovery enabled him to take up some literary projects. During the thirties his heavy correspondence had left him little time for other sorts of writing. After the accident he stopped answering letters and began to revise the major *Arya* series for publication as books. He gave priority to *The Life Divine*. The revised version of the first of its two 'books' was published in 1939. The next year the second 'book', completely recast and with the addition of several new chapters, was issued in two volumes. *The Life Divine* soon attracted favourable attention. In 1941 S. K. Maitra, head of the department of philosophy of Banaras Hindu University, published a pioneer study that remains one of the best brief expositions of Sri Aurobindo's thought. Maitra concluded that Sri Aurobindo 'has perhaps no equal in breadth and comprehensiveness of outlook in the whole range of the history of philosophy. The only philosophers who can be compared with him in this respect are Plato and Hegel in the Western world and Shankara in our land.'[2] This appraisal was echoed, albeit 'with diffidence', by D. L. Murray, editor of the *Times Literary Supplement*, who said that Sri Aurobindo might prove to be one of those rare 'truly creative philosophers' who have given 'a new thought and a new vision to mankind'—among whom Murray included only Plato, Berkeley, Kant, Hegel, and Bergson.[3] In 1942 the *TLS* published a favourable review of *The Life Divine* by Sir Francis Younghusband, the British explorer, administrator and writer who had himself had mystical experiences. The previous year Younghusband had written in a private letter that he considered *The Life Divine* to be 'the greatest book which has been produced in my time'.[4] Sri Aurobindo's reputation as a philosopher has remained high in the country of his birth.[5] In the West he is little known in academic circles, though in recent years there have been signs of increased interest in his writings in the United States.[6]

In the years that followed the publication of *The Life Divine*, Sri Aurobindo worked on revised versions of his other major prose works, *The Synthesis of Yoga* (first part only), *The Human Cycle*, and *The Ideal of Human Unity*. The first editions of these books came out in 1948, 1949, and 1950. But most of his literary energy during this period went into *Savitri*. Repeatedly revising most of its forty-nine cantos, he transformed the poem from an extended symbolic narrative into a repository of yogic knowledge and vision. The first volume of *Savitri* was published in 1950, the remainder in 1951. Sri Aurobindo's poetical works have found many admirers, especially among those interested in his yoga. Critical opinion in India has from the first been sharply divided.[7] A few writers have championed Sri Aurobindo as the foremost Indo-Anglian poet, the initiator of a new age of spiritual inspiration. Others have found little poetic merit in his work, whatever its value as an expression of mystical experience. 'Esoteric spiritual significance will be claimed for these poems—the literary reviewer cannot reach there', was one early opinion.[8] No Western critic of stature has shown interest in Sri Aurobindo's poetry, but a few American writers have been struck by its evocative power, one going so far as to proclaim *Savitri* 'perhaps the most powerful artistic work in the world for expanding man's mind towards the Absolute'.[9]

Sri Aurobindo's daily routine included a close reading of the newspaper. During the late thirties, most news of world affairs was bad. When the War broke out, Sri Aurobindo saw it as a reflection on the physical plane of the struggle between the forces of light and darkness that he and the Mother were engaged in on the spiritual level. Hitler's Germany, he said, had become 'possessed' by those forces of evil that are figured in the Indian tradition as *asuras*. The Allied nations, hardly godlike in themselves, had become, through their opposition to the Axis dictatorships, representatives of the *daiva* or divine forces.* In September 1940 Sri Aurobindo publicly announced his support of France and Britain. This came as a shock to many in India. How could one who had fought, and encouraged others to fight, against British imperialism, now proclaim his adhesion to the British cause? Sri Aurobindo's attitude towards the Indian struggle for freedom had not changed, but he saw the War as a matter of greater moment for the world as a whole as well as for India itself. If the British Empire was destroyed by Japan and Germany, the result for India would be not liberation but a harsher servitude.

In 1942, while Japanese troops were approaching the Indo-Burmese border, Sir Stafford Cripps, a member of the British War Cabinet, flew to Delhi with a proposal for India's leaders: independence after the war in exchange for co-operation with the Allied effort. Sri Aurobindo saw the Cripps Offer as a means for India to combine its national and global imperatives. Acceptance would enable the country to defend itself effectively, and later 'to determine for herself, and organise in all liberty of choice, her freedom and unity'.[10] Sri Aurobindo's views, sent by telegram to Cripps, and conveyed to the Congress Working Committee by messenger, had no influence on the negotiations in Delhi. The Offer was rejected and subsequent events, which acceptance might have

---

* This may seem to some readers to be an unnecessarily supernatural explanation of a dirty bloody war; but it at least has the virtue of making the diabolism—what else can it be called?—of Buchenwald and Auschwitz comprehensible.

precluded, made the partition of India inevitable. In a message delivered on the eve of independence in August 1947 Sri Aurobindo regreted the political division of the subcontinent as a source of weakness and hindrance to prosperity. Looking to the positive side he regarded 'the birthday of free India' as 'the beginning of a new age' for the country and for the world. India had a great role to play in the resurgence of Asia and in the development of an inner and outer world-union, but more important it had a 'spiritual gift' that could be of decisive importance to humanity as it prepared to take a step forward in evolution.[11]

By this time Sri Aurobindo's fame as a yogin and philosopher had spread throughout India, and penetrated Europe and America. An increasing number of people came for his darshans, which after the accident of 1938 were given on four instead of three occasions yearly. His growing celebrity occasionally took strange forms. A crude picture of him was printed on dhotis manufactured by the Aravind Mill, which made him look, he commented wryly, 'like a criminal or a lunatic.'[12] Distortions of a different sort were circulated in the form of popular legends. It was thought by many that Sri Aurobindo spent much of his time in levitation, that he could fly, that he lived in a cellar and ate food lowered down to him in a bucket, that he spoke twenty-eight languages. There was little he could do to combat such canards; but when supposedly factual biographical articles and books began to be published that misrepresented events in his past, he felt obliged, 'for the sake of truth', to set the record straight.*

After independence Sri Aurobindo relaxed his rule of over twenty years and gave personal interviews to representatives of the French and the Indian governments. In September 1947 Maurice Schumann, a French diplomat, and François Baron, the Governor of French India, spoke to Sri Aurobindo about a planned Indo-French cultural institution they wished to set up in Pondicherry under his direction. In 1950 K. M. Munshi, an Indian Cabinet Minister, and the Maharaja of Bhavnagar, then Governor of the state of Madras, paid separate calls. Munshi, a student of Sri Aurobindo's at Baroda College, and an enthusiastic reader of

---

* The notes in which Sri Aurobindo confuted these statements form an important body of information on his life, and they have been used and quoted from freely in this as in all other biographies. Many of the notes were written in the third person because they were not intended to be published over his signature.

Bande Mataram and later of *The Life Divine*, left a vivid account of his meeting. Seeing his old teacher 'after the lapse of more than 40 years', Munshi, a hard-nosed politician, was struck by his extraordinary appearance: 'I saw before me a being completely transformed, radiant, blissful, enveloped in an atmosphere of godlike calm. He spoke in a low clear voice, which stirred the depths of my being.' Munshi told Sri Aurobindo of the conflict he felt between the call of duty and the urge to make spiritual progress. Sri Aurobindo told him: 'You need not give up the world in order to advance in self-realization.' The two then spoke on current political questions: the Hindu legal code, the Indo-Pakistan situation, the status of Pondicherry. On parting, Munshi asked Sri Aurobindo when he would come out from his retirement. Sri Aurobindo replied: 'I cannot say. I must first complete my work here.'[13]

In 1948 and 1950 Sri Aurobindo was the recipient of two Indian awards: the Catamanchi Ramalinga Reddi National Prize, awarded by the Andhra University, and the Asiatic Society Medal for Peace and Culture. Around this time a concerted effort was made to have him awarded the Nobel Prize for literature. Sir Francis Younghusband and the novelist Aldous Huxley, who considered *The Life Divine* 'a book not merely of the highest importance as regards its content, but remarkably fine as a piece of philosophic and religious literature',[14] had already written on Sri Aurobindo's behalf. In 1949 two Nobel Laureates, Gabriela Mistral and Pearl S. Buck, moved and seconded a formal nomination to the Swedish Academy. Their proposal was supported by a memorial signed by three dozen heads of Indian governmental, educational and cultural bodies. The Swedish Academy considered the nomination for the prize of 1950, the last year of Sri Aurobindo's life.

Late in the 1940s Sri Aurobindo showed signs of prostatic enlargement. Not long afterwards there was a remission of the symptoms, but in mid 1950 they reappeared in force. The complication most to be feared in cases of hyperplasia of the prostate is kidney infection leading to uraemia. This condition set in towards the close of the year. A dedicated team of physicians was in attendance but Sri Aurobindo declined to receive any major treatment, or even to use his therapeutic power on himself. Asked why, he said simply, 'Can't explain; you won't understand.'[15] He fell into what the doctors assumed to be a terminal uraemic coma; but it was a strange sort of coma, from which the patient seemed able to emerge at will. During his periods of full outward awareness Sri Aurobindo spoke to his attendants, and even, when the end drew near, kissed these faithful companions of his last years. Some time after midnight on 5 December 1950 he plunged within for the last time, and at 1.26 A.M. his vital functions ceased.

Epilogue

Reports of Sri Aurobindo's passing appeared on the front page of the major newspapers of India on 6 December 1950. For more than a week, follow-up stories and tributes continued to fill them 'to the exclusion of much ordinary news'. (News coverage focussed on the deteriorating situation in Korea. Several commentators remarked that Sri Aurobindo's death seemed especially inauspicious at a moment 'when humanity is in danger of being engulfed in yet another hideous war'.) Most of the country's leading public figures issued memorial messages that have a ring of sincerity rarely met with in official panegyrics. Prime Minister Nehru remembered Sri Aurobindo as 'one of the greatest minds of our generation'. Sardar Patel, who would survive him by only ten days, spoke of his efforts 'in the mystic field of the struggle of the spirit and the flesh' in which he 'attained a rare triumph of mind over matter' while never losing his absorbing interest 'in our problems and fortunes'. The philosopher and statesman Dr S. Radhakrishnan lauded Sri Aurobindo as 'the greatest intellectual of our age' and as 'a major force for the life of spirit'.

Among the many obituaries published as lead editorials in Indian papers on 6 December, that of *The Times of India* may be taken as representative. After giving an account of Sri Aurobindo's career, the writer commented:

It is a romantic story but in Aurobindo himself there was nothing of the romancer. By nature introspective, he had also a strong streak of the iconoclast in his being. From early life Aurobindo sought to break new ground and reach out to new frontiers. A man of such mental intensity was inevitably something of an idealist, but just as his poetry was often a lyrical instrument for his philosophy so also his mysticism was in some ways peculiarly practical. For a recluse he was remarkably interested in and informed on politics. And it is perhaps typical of his strongly individualistic mind that his views on mundane affairs more often than not bordered on the controversial.... The world to him was the abode of a spiritual evolution which manifested itself progressively in higher and higher forms of conscience as the mind reached out to the uplands of supreme thought.

Not surprisingly the obituary published in *The Times* (London) on the 6th devoted most of its four paragraphs to Sri Aurobindo's scholastic and political career; but it also mentioned his publications, in particular *The Life Divine*, which had made him 'widely known in the west', and concluded with an affirmation of his 'significance and importance'.

Sri Aurobindo's funeral, originally scheduled for 6 December, was not held until the 9th. This made it possible for tens of thousands of devotees, admirers, and others to have a last *darshan*. Many of the devotees who filed past his body reported seeing a tangible aura of light surrounding it. Even the correspondent of a major Calcutta newspaper wrote on the 7th: 'The body of Sri Aurobindo is lying majestically on his bed, a marvel of radiance, without any sign that there was no life in it.'[1] Reports of this nature do not lend themselves to objective verification; but the remarkable state of preservation of Sri Aurobindo's body even fifty-five hours after his death was certified by a team of physicians. On 7 December, three of Sri Aurobindo's doctor-disciples, led by Dr P. Sanyal of the Calcutta Medical College, together with Dr V. P. Barbet, head of the General Hospital of Pondicherry, examined the body and found no sign of putrefaction, decomposition or suggillation (livid marks). 'The Body is in perfect condition of repose as I found the first day of death', wrote Sanyal. Barbet concurred with his Indian colleagues and allowed the interment to be postponed beyond the forty-eight-hour limit in force in French India. Asked by a reporter for his opinion of the phenomenon, Barbet replied bluntly, 'I don't make any declaration.'[2] According to the Mother, the preservation and luminosity of the body were a result of Sri Aurobindo's sadhana. In a message issued on the 7th, she wrote, 'Sri Aurobindo's body is charged with such concentration of supramental light that there is no sign of decomposition and the body will be kept on his bed as long as it remains intact.'[3]

The first signs of decomposition appeared on 8 December. The next day Sri Aurobindo's body was placed in a silver-lined rosewood coffin that was lowered into a samadhi or vault in the courtyard of the main building of the ashram. The Mother issued a message for the occasion that later was engraved on a marble slab that was attached to the side of the samadhi:

To Thee who hast been the material envelope of our Master, to Thee our infinite gratitude. Before Thee who hast done so much for us, who hast worked, struggled, suffered, hoped, endured so much, before Thee who hast willed all, attempted all, prepared, achieved all for us, before Thee we bow down and implore that we may never forget, even for a moment, all we owe to Thee.[4]

Sri Aurobindo's disciples were at first shocked, then overcome with sorrow at his unexpected departure. The Mother encouraged them to lay their grief aside and to look forward. It was 'left to us', she wrote, 'to realise his work with all the sincerity, eagerness and concentration necessary'.[5] Since 1950 the Sri Aurobindo Ashram has grown into a large and diversified spiritual community. The Mother oversaw its development and guided the inner and outer lives of the disciples until her passing in 1973. For a number of years before that she was much occupied with Auroville, an 'international township' that was inaugurated on marginal land outside Pondicherry in 1968. Many parts of this desert have become green, as settlers from different parts of India and many foreign countries have built houses, planted trees and begun agricultural and small industrial ventures. In 1975 the settlers came into conflict with the legal custodians of the land. The Government of India intervened, and after a period of direct stewardship vested the title of the land in an independent Auroville Foundation. This body consists of a governing board of prominent citizens, an assembly of residents, who remain practically autonomous, and an international advisory council, whose purpose is to encourage and promote the development of Auroville in accordance with its Charter, a document written by the Mother in February 1968:

1) Auroville belongs to nobody in particular. Auroville belongs to humanity as a whole.
But to live in Auroville one must be the willing servitor of the Divine Consciousness.
2) Auroville will be the place of an unending education, of constant progress, and a youth that never ages.
3) Auroville wants to be the bridge between the past and the future.
Taking advantage of all discoveries from without and from within, Auroville will boldly spring towards future realisations.

4) Auroville will be a site of material and spiritual researches for a living embodiment of an actual human unity.[6]

Sri Aurobindo never imagined that the ultimate goal of his yoga— a divine life, on earth, of transformed individuals joined together in a 'gnostic society'—could be achieved with miraculous rapidity. Nor did he look forward to a day when a multitude of people would practice his method of yoga. 'Nothing depends on the numbers,' he once wrote a disciple. 'The numbers of Buddhism or Christianity were so great because the majority professed it as a creed without its making the least difference to their external life. If the new consciousness were satisfied with that, it could also and much more easily command homage and acceptance by the whole earth. It is because it is a greater consciousness, the Truth-Consciousness, that it will insist on a real change.'[7]

The transformation that Sri Aurobindo envisaged was not an amelioration of existing terrestrial conditions, but rather a 'radical change in the earth-consciousness'. This could not be effected by altering 'social matters within the frame of the present humanity', but by bringing down 'a higher spiritual light and power'.[8] For many, talk of spiritual light and power in the face of the over-whelming problems of contemporary humanity is indicative, if not of simple delusion, then of badly arranged priorities. Sri Auro-bindo anticipated this line of criticism. He knew that the 'prevalent mentality' of mankind believed that the 'spiritual tendency . . . has come to very little', and that the spiritual man 'confuses the plain practical and vital issues life puts before us'. But he was convinced that such criticism missed the mark. The work of spirituality was not 'to solve human problems on the past or present mental basis, but to create a new foundation of our being and our life and knowledge'. Without this radically new foundation, no mental solution could give lasting results:

Spirituality cannot be called upon to deal with life by a non-spiritual method or attempt to cure its ills by the panaceas, the political, social or other mechanical remedies which the mind is constantly attempting and which have always failed and will continue to fail to solve anything. The most drastic changes made by these means change nothing; for the old ills exist in a new form: the aspect of the outward environment is altered, but man remains what he was. . . . Only a spiritual change, an evolution of his being from the superficial mental towards the deeper spiritual conscious-ness, can make a real and effective difference.[9]

Sri Aurobindo did not belittle attempts to improve the economic and social condition of man. No representative of the Eastern spiritual tradition has given more importance to human society. He considered the individual and the group to be interdependent, but he assigned a certain priority to the individual as the agent of evolutionary change. The principal object of society was 'to provide the conditions of life and growth by which individual Man,—not isolated men or a class or a privileged race, but all individual men according to their capacity,—and the race through the growth of its individuals may travel towards this divine perfection.' 'A perfect human world', he wrote elsewhere, 'cannot be created by men or composed of men who are themselves imperfect.'[10]

What contemporary humanity really needs is not the final victory of one ideology over all the others, but a united human endeavour based on a harmony of different world-views. A major step in this direction would be the integration of the two principal ways of regarding existence—the spirituality preserved in the religious traditions of the East, and the practicality represented by the political and economic systems of the West. Sri Aurobindo looked forward to this when he wrote in 1916:

The most vital issue of the age is whether the future progress of humanity is to be governed by the modern economic and materialistic mind of the West or by a nobler pragmatism guided, uplifted and enlightened by spiritual culture and knowledge. . . . The hope of the world lies in the re-arousing in the East of the old spiritual practicality and large and profound vision and power of organisation under the insistent contact of the West and in the flooding out of the light of Asia on the Occident, no longer in forms that are now static, effete, unadaptive, but in new forms stirred, dynamic and effective.[11]

The work of Sri Aurobindo may be looked on as an attempt to re-establish under modern conditions the 'spiritual practicality' that he regarded as the great discovery of ancient India. Such an effort, he felt, would be a movement not of reaction, but of renewal and cyclic progression. 'The traditions of the past are very great in their own place, in the past,' he wrote in a notable letter, 'but I do not see why we should merely repeat them and not go farther. In the spiritual development of the consciousness upon earth the great past ought to be followed by a greater future.'[12]

Bibliography

Bibliography

I. PRINCIPAL DOCUMENTARY SOURCES

Papers of Sri Aurobindo (Sri Aurobindo Ashram Archives and Research Library, Pondicherry).

Collection of biographical documents at Sri Aurobindo Ashram Archives and Research Library.

Records of St Paul's School; records of Kings's College and of Cambridge University; records of the Civil Service Commission (India Office Records, London).

Records of Baroda State (Baroda Record Office, Gujarat State Archives); records of Baroda College (Maharaja Sayajirao University, Baroda).

Records of Government of India, Home Department (National Archives, New Delhi); records of Government of Bengal (West Bengal State Archives, Calcutta); records of Government of Madras (Tamil Nadu State Archives, Madras).

II. WORKS OF SRI AUROBINDO

Between 1971 and 1973 all previously published works of Sri Aurobindo were issued in a uniform series of 29 volumes entitled *Sri Aurobindo Birth Centenary Library:*

Volume 1. *Bande Mataram: Early Political Writings–I.*
Volume 2. *Karmayogin: Early Political Writings–II.*
Volume 3. *The Harmony of Virtue: Early Cultural Writings.*
Volume 4. *Bangla Rachana* [Writings in Bengali].
Volume 5. *Collected Poems: The Complete Poetical Works.*
Volume 6. *Collected Plays and Short Stories* [I].
Volume 7. *Collected Plays and Short Stories* [II].
Volume 8. *Translations from Sanskrit and Other Languages.*
Volume 9. *The Future Poetry.*
Volume 10. *The Secret of the Veda.*
Volume 11. *Hymns to the Mystic Fire.*
Volume 12. *The Upanishads: Texts, Translations and Commentaries.*
Volume 13. *Essays on the Gita.*
Volume 14. *The Foundations of Indian Culture* and *The Renaissance in India.*

Volume 15.   *Social and Political Thought* [includes *The Human Cycle*,
             The Ideal of Human Unity, War and Self Determination].
Volume 16.   *The Supramental Manifestation and Other Writings*.
Volume 17.   *The Hour of God and Other Writings*.
Volume 18.   *The Life Divine* [I].
Volume 19.   *The Life Divine* [II].
Volume 20.   *The Synthesis of Yoga* [I].
Volume 21.   *The Synthesis of Yoga* [II].
Volume 22.   *Letters on Yoga* [I].
Volume 23.   *Letters on Yoga* [II].
Volume 24.   *Letters on Yoga* [III].
Volume 25.   *The Mother* with *Letters on the Mother* and [translations of
             the Mother's] *Prayers and Meditations*.
Volume 26.   *On Himself: Compiled from Notes and Letters*.
Volume 27.   *Supplement*.
Volume 28.   *Savitri: A Legend and a Symbol* [I].
Volume 29.   *Savitri: A Legend and a Symbol* [II].

Since 1977 works by Sri Aurobindo not included in the Centenary Library
have appeared in *Sri Aurobindo: Archives and Research*, a semi-annual
journal published by Sri Aurobindo Ashram Trust.

Letters on Yoga (Centenary Library Volumes 22–4) is a selection from Sri
Aurobindo's correspondence of the 1930s. Many letters not included in
Letters on Yoga may be found in compilations by disciples, e.g.:

Nirodbaran's Correspondence with Sri Aurobindo: The Complete Set. Two
    volumes. Pondicherry, Sri Aurobindo Ashram Trust, 1983.
Dilip Kumar Roy. *Sri Aurobindo Came to Me*. Pondicherry, Sri Auro-
    bindo Ashram, 1952.

Several of Sri Aurobindo's disciples kept written records of his talks, and
later published edited versions of these records. The principal published
versions are:

Nirodbaran, ed. *Talks with Sri Aurobindo*. First volume, Calcutta: Sri
    Aurobindo Pathamandir, 1966; subsequent volumes, Pondicherry:
    Sri Aurobindo Ashram Trust.
A. B. Purani, ed. *Evening Talks with Sri Aurobindo*. Complete in One
    Volume. Pondicherry: Sri Aurobindo Ashram Trust, 1982.

III. BIOGRAPHIES OF SRI AUROBINDO

Only works containing a significant amount of original
material (see Preface) are listed here.

K. R. Srinivasa Iyengar. *Sri Aurobindo*. Calcutta: Arya Publishing
    House, 1945; second edition, 1950; third (revised and enlarged)
    edition, subtitled 'A Biography and a History', published by Sri

Aurobindo Internationai Centre of Education, 1972; fourth (revised) edition, 1985.

G. E. Monod-Herzen. *Shri Aurobindo*. Pondicherry, Sri Aurobindo Ashram, 1954; second edition, 1983.

Nirodbaran. *Twelve Years with Sri Aurobindo*. Pondicherry, Sri Aurobindo Ashram Trust, 1972; second and third editions 1973 and 1988.

A. B. Purani. *The Life of Sri Aurobindo*. Pondicherry: Sri Aurobindo Ashram, 1958; second and third editions, 1960 and 1964; fourth (revised and enlarged) edition, 1978; reprinted 1987.

Girijashankar Raychaudhuri. *Sriarabinda o Banglay Svadeshi Yug*. Calcutta: Navabharat Publishers, 1956.

The journal *Sri Aurobindo: Archives and Research* (Pondicherry: Sri Aurobindo Ashram Trust, 1977–) contains verbatim reprints of biographical documents, and articles of biographical interest by the author of the present book.

IV. OTHER WORKS CITED

Bannerji, Jitendralal. 'Aravinda Ghosh—A Study'. *Modern Review* 6 (1909): 476–87.

Binyon, Laurence. 'Introductory Memoir'. In *Songs of Love and Death* by Manmohan Ghose. Calcutta: University of Calcutta, 1968.

Bipan Chandra. *Modern India*. New Delhi: National Council of Educational Research and Training, 1984.

Bose, Bejoy Krishna, ed. *The Alipore Bomb Trial*. Calcutta: Butterworth & Co., 1922.

Chakrabarti, Basanti. 'Amader Aurodada' [Our Aurodada]. *Galpa Bharati* 6 (1357 Bengali era): 776–85.

Chandwani, P. B. 'Sri Aurobindo—A Few Reminiscences'. *Mother India* 23 (1971): 468–9.

Chirol, Valentine. *Indian Unrest*. Macmillan and Co., 1910.

Cousins, James H. *New Ways in English Literature*. Madras: Ganesh & Co., n.d. (1917).

David-Néel, Alexandra. *Journal de Voyage: Lettres à son Mari*. Paris: Plon, 1975.

De, Brajendranath. 'Reminiscences of an Indian Member of the Indian Civil Service'–XI. *The Calcutta Review* 132 (1954): 178–82.

Deb, Suresh Chandra. 'Sri Aurobindo as I Knew Him'. *Mother India* 2(13) (15 August 1950): unpaged.

Gaekwar, Sayajirao. *Speeches & Addresses of His Highness Sayaji Rao III, Maharaja of Baroda*. Volume One 1877–1910. Cambridge: Privately Printed at the University Press, 1927.

Gilbert, Martin. *Servant of India: A Study of Imperial Rule from 1905–1910*. London: Longmans, 1966.

Gordon, Leonard A. *Bengal: The Nationalist Movement 1876–1940*. New Delhi: Manohar, 1979.

Ghose, Barindrakumar. 'Sri Aurobindo (As I Understand Him)'. Unpublished MS.

Ker, James Campbell. *Political Trouble in India 1907–1917*. Calcutta: Editions Indian, 1973 (reprint of the Calcutta edition of 1917).

Kopf, David. *The Brahmo Samaj and the Shaping of the Modern Indian Mind*. Princeton, New Jersey: Princeton University Press, 1979.

Madan Gopal, ed. *The Life and Times of Subhas Chandra Bose: as told in his own words*. New Delhi: Vikas Publishing House Pvt. Ltd., 1978.

Minto, Mary, Countess of. *India: Minto and Morley 1905–1910*. London: Macmillan and Co., Ltd., 1934.

Maitra, S. K. *An Introduction to the Philosophy of Sri Aurobindo*. Calcutta: The Culture Publishers, 1941.

Mother, the. *Collected Works of the Mother*. Seventeen volumes. Pondicherry: Sri Aurobindo Ashram Trust, 1978–89.

Mukerjee, Hirendranath. *India's Struggle for Freedom*. Calcutta: National Book Agency Private Limited, 1962.

Munshi, K. M. 'Kulapati's Letter', *Bhavan's Journal* 8(26) (1962): 8–9.

———. 'Aurobindo Ashram—A Pilgrimage'. The Hindustan Times Independence Supplement. 15 August 1952.

Nandy, Ashis. *The Intimate Enemy: Loss and Recovery of Self under Colonialism*. Delhi: Oxford University Press, 1988.

Nevinson, Henry W. *The New Spirit in India*. Delhi: Metropolitan Book Co., 1975 (reprint of the London edition of 1909).

———. *Fire of Life*. London: James Nesbet & Co., 1935.

Organ, Troy. Book review. *Philosophy East & West* 26 (1976): 352–6.

———. 'Rejoinder to Robert A. McDermott's Reply'. *Philosophy East & West* 26 (1976): 489–92.

Piper, Raymond, *The Hungry Eye*. Los Angeles: De Vorss & Co., 1952.

Rowlatt, Justice S. A. T. et al. *Report of Committee Appointed to Investigate Revolutionary Conspiracies in India*. London: His Majesty's Stationary Office, 1918.

Sergeant, Philip. *The Ruler of Baroda*. London: John Murray, 1928.

Singh, Karan. *Prophet of Indian Nationalism*. With a Foreword by Jawaharlal Nehru. Bombay: Bharatiya Vidya Bhavan, 1967.

Trivedi, A. K., ed. *The Baroda College Golden Jubilee Commemoration Volume*. Bombay: The Times of India Press, 1933.

Reference Notes

Written works of Sri Aurobindo are referred to by short title of book or title of periodical (generally abbreviated) only. Full titles are given in part II of the Bibliography. Letters published in *Letters on Yoga* are not dated; letters published elsewhere generally are. See part II of the Bibliography for details on the publication of Sri Aurobindo's letters. Sri Aurobindo's talks are referred to by date; a reference also is given to a work in which the reader may find a printed transcription. These transcriptions sometimes are defective; the author has in a few places emended accidentals such as capitalization and punctuation. Works by authors other than Sri Aurobindo are referred to by author's name, and (when necessary) short title. See part IV of the Bibliography for details on these works.

The following abbreviations have been used:

A&R	*Sri Aurobindo: Archives and Research*
GOB	Government of Bengal
GOI	Government of India
HD	Home Department (series A, B, D)
IOR	India Office Records
NAI	National Archives of India
NMML	Nehru Memorial Museum and Library
Pol. conf.	political confidential (file)
q.	quoted in
SAAA	Sri Aurobindo Ashram Archives
WBSA	West Bengal State Archives

PREFACE

1 Nandy 85.
2 Gordon 102, 106.
3 Ibid. 101; Gordon cites some pertinent examples in a note.
4 Ibid.

CHAPTER 1
INDIAN ORIGINS

1 Letter of 3 June 1935, published in *Nirodbaran's Correspondence with Sri Aurobindo* 253.
2 *The Supramental Manifestation* 102.

3   Ibid. 260; *A&R* 5 (1981): 44.
4   Rajnarain Bose, q. Kopf 67.
5   Letter of Sri Aurobindo, q. Dilip
    Kumar Roy 319.
6   Letter Manmohan Ghose to
    Laurence Binyon 18 February
    1888. Binyon papers (photocopy
    SAAA).
7   Chakrabarti 778 (in English in
    text).
8   *On Himself* 1

CHAPTER 2
EDUCATION IN ENGLAND

1   *A&R* 9 (1985): 128–9, 193.
2   Talk of 28 June 1926, published in
    Purani, *Evening Talks* 378.
3   *On Himself* 3–4.
4   Talk of 30 December 1938,
    published in Purani, *Evening
    Talks* 203.
5   *On Himself* 1.
6   A. Wood, note in GOI HP-D,
    June 1908, 13, 3; Binyon 4;
    Sergeant 140n.
7   *On Himself* 17; letter to Mrinalini
    Ghose 30 August 1905, translated
    from Bengali in Purani, *Life*
    (1978): 82; *On Himself* 4.
8   *A&R* 1(2) (December 1977): 88.
9   A. Wood, note in GOI HP-D
    June 1908, 13, 3.
10 *On Himself* 2.
11 *The Harmony of Virtue* 130–1.
12 *Bande Mataram* 53.
13 *The Harmony of Virtue* 8.
14 Letter K. D. Ghose to
    Jogindranath Bose 2 December
    1890 (photocopy SAAA).
15 Letter G. W. Prothero 20
    November 1892. IOR J&P
    1966/92, reproduced in Purani,
    Life (1978): 328.
16 *On Himself* 2.
17 IOR V/7/212: 5.
18 Memorandum by Senior
    Examiner, Civil Service
    Commission, 16 November 1892.

IOR J&P 1966/92, reproduced in
    Purani, *Life* (1978): 323.
19 Undated oral account (1940s),
    published in *Mother India* 23
    (1971): 102.
20 Talk of 12 December 1940,
    published in *Mother India* 39
    (1986): 270.
21 Letter Lord Kimberley 2
    December 1892, IOR J&P
    1966/92, reproduced in Purani,
    Life (1978): 335.
22 Lord Kimberley, q. Bipan
    Chandra 158.
23 *A&R* 1(2) (December 1977): 88;
    Talk of 28 June 1926,
    incompletely published in Purani,
    Evening Talks 378.
24 De 181.

CHAPTER 3
CAREER AND FAMILY LIFE

1   M. K. Sharangpani, in Trivedi,
    ed., *Golden Jubilee* 39.
2   M. V. Purohit, letter 25 February
    1968 (SAAA).
3   Talk of 30 December 1938:
    Purani, *Evening Talks* 203.
4   Ibid.
5   *On Himself* 31.
6   Unpublished talk of 1 July 1926
    (SAAA).
7   Ibid.
8   M. H. Kantavala, in Trivedi, ed.,
    Golden Jubilee 24; S. B.
    Didmishe, letter 18 September
    1967, reproduced in *A&R* 2
    (1978): 204.
9   Gaekwar 83; identified by Sri
    Aurobindo as written by him in
    talk of 12 December 1940,
    published in *Mother India* 39
    (1986): 269.
10 *On Himself* 9.
11 S. B. Didmishe, in *A&R* 2 (1978):
    204; Munshi, 'Kulapati's Letter' 9.
12 Munshi, 'Kulapati's Letter' 8.
13 Chandwani 469, 468.

14 Letter K. D. Ghose to Jogindranath Bose 2 December 1890 (photocopy SAAA).
15 Barindrakumar Ghose MS 11 (SAAA).
16 Chakrabarti 776–7 (translated from Bengali).
17 *A&R* 1(2) (December 1977): 85.

CHAPTER 4
A POET AND A POLITICIAN

1 *On Himself* 374.
2 *A&R* 12 (1988): 173–4.
3 *Bande Mataram* 15.
4 Ibid. 22, 26, 8.
5 Ibid. 13, 12.
6 *A&R* 7 (1983): 166.
7 Unpublished talk of 1 July 1926 (SAAA); *Bande Mataram* 658.
8 *Bande Mataram* 57–8.
9 Gaekwar 90; *Congress Presidential Addresses* 619; *On Himself* 25.
10 *The Harmony of Virtue* 98, 101.
11 Ibid. 100.
12 Ibid. 142.
13 Ibid. 180.
14 Ibid. 174.
15 Ibid. 176.
16 Unpublished portion of 'Notes on the Mahabharata' (SAAA).
17 *A&R* 1(1) (April 1977): 31.
18 *The Upanishads* 466.
19 *On Himself* 98.
20 Talk of 22 June 1926, published in Purani, *Evening Talks* 405.
21 Ker 128.
22 Rowlatt Report, paragraph 30; see also Chirol *passim*.

CHAPTER 5
BANDE MATARAM

1 *Bande Mataram* 22.
2 Deb (unpaged).
3 Ibid.
4 Chintamani, q. Mukerjee 113.
5 *Bande Mataram* 86.
6 Diary of G. S. Khaparde, 31 December 1906 (NAI).

7 Letter Bhupendranath Bose to Pherozshah Mehta 14 January 1907, Pherozshah Mehta papers (NMML).
8 Diary of Dunlop Smith, 20 March 1907, q. Gilbert 77.
9 Letter Lord Minto to Lord Morley 19 March 1907, q. Countess of Minto 109.
10 *Supplement* 49.
11 *On Himself* 375.
12 Nevinson, *Fire of Life* 232–3; Nevinson, *New Spirit* 220–6.
13 Barindrakumar Ghose MS 45 (SAAA).
14 Letter Tilak to Motilal Ghose 2 December 1907 (photocopy SAAA).
15 *On Himself* 49.
16 Talk of 17 February 1940, published in Nirodbaran *Talks* ii. 194.
17 *On Himself* 49.
18 *On Himself* 48.
19 Ibid.
20 *Bande Mataram* 871–2.

CHAPTER 6
WAGING WAR AGAINST THE KING

1 *On Himself* 22.
2 *A&R* 3 (1979): 4, 3.
3 *A&R* 1(2) (December 1977): 3–4.
4 *On Himself* 24.
5 *Jugantar* 17 June 1906, translation from Report on Native Newspapers in Bengal, week ending 23 June 1906 (WBSA).
6 *Jugantar* 26 August 1906, translation from WBSA, Freedom Movement Papers, file 104.
7 GOI HD-A September 1910, 33–40, 18.
8 Talk of 18 December 1938: published in Nirodbaran, *Talks* i. 58.
9 GOB pol. conf. 266 of 1908.
10 GOI HD-A. May 1908. 104–11, 2.

11 Barindrakumar Ghose to Girijashankar Raychaudhuri, q. Raychaudhuri 670.

12 For the 'Sweets Letter', 'Scribblings', etc. see *A&R* 5 (1981): 205–7; portions of the judgment are reproduced in *A&R* 6 (1982): 221–7.

13 *Bangla Rachana* 270, 276–8 (translated from Bengali).

14 C. R. Das, q. Bijoy Krishna Bose, ed., *The Alipore Bomb Trial* 140–1.

CHAPTER 7
KARMAYOGIN

1 Talk of 13 April 1923, unpublished transcript (SAAA).

2 *Karmayogin* 11, 14, 17, 16–17.

3 Ibid. 19, 9.

4 Ibid. 19.

5 Ibid. 9.

6 Ibid. 343.

7 Ibid. 355; *The Hour of God* 378–9, 382–7.

8 *The Harmony of Virtue* 345.

9 Bombay Presidency Abstract of Intelligence, reproduced in *A&R* 1(1) (April 1977): 2.

10 Talks of 5 and 21 January 1939, published in Nirodbaran, *Talks* i. 168, 290.

11 *Letters on Yoga* 1385–6.

12 Bannerji 487.

13 *Karmayogin* 3–4.

14 Ibid. 61–2.

15 Talk of 14 March 1924, q. Purani, *Life* (1978): 124.

16 Various documents, cited *A&R* 7 (1983): 89–90.

17 GOB pol. conf. 205 of 1909, reproduced *A&R* 7 (1983): 71–86.

18 GOI HD-A. October 1909, 230–43.

19 Ibid.; GOB pol. conf. 205 of 1909.

20 Ibid. (both).

21 Talk of 6 January 1939, published in Nirodbaran, *Talks* i. 172.

22 GOI HD-B. November 1909, 103–4, reproduced *A&R* 7 (1983): 207.

23 Undated fragmentary letter published in *Sri Aurobindo's Action* 6(4&5) (February/March 1976): 4.

24 *Karmayogin* 324, 326, 328.

25 *On Himself* 36.

26 Ibid. 37.

27 *A&R* 9 (1985): 69.

28 *On Himself* 423.

29 Ibid. 37, 34.

30 Madan Gopal, ed. 42.

31 Nehru, Foreword to Singh.

CHAPTER 8
EARLY YEARS
IN PONDICHERRY

1 Letter Alexandra David-Néel to her husband 27 November 1911, published in *Journal de Voyage* 68 (translated from French).

2 *Supplement* 426.

3 Ibid. 425, 427.

4 *A&R* 8 (1984): 61.

5 *A&R* 5 (1981): 186–7.

6 *Supplement* 455.

7 *The Synthesis of Yoga* 320.

8 Talk of 1924, published in Purani, *Life* (1978): 152.

9 Letter Alexandra David-Néel to her husband 27 November 1911, published in *Journal de Voyage* 69 (translated from French).

10 Letter to Bhupal Chandra Bose 19 February 1919, published in *Supplement* 422.

11 Letter to Joseph Baptista 5 January 1920, published in *On Himself* 430.

12 Ibid. 431.

13 *The Hour of God* 366.

14 Letter to Dr Moonje 30 August 1920, published in *On Himself* 432–3.

15 Letter to Barindrakumar Ghose, published in *A&R* 4 (1980): 13, 23 (translated from Bengali).

CHAPTER 9
BRAHMAN AND VASUDEVA

1 *Letters on Yoga* 428.
2 *On Himself* 378.
3 Ibid. 50.
4 Undated talk published in *Sri Aurobindo Circle* 42 (1986): 46; Talk of 12 December 1940, published in *Mother India* 39 (1986): 269; cf. *Letters on Yoga* 747; *The Synthesis of Yoga* 517n.
5 *On His. self* 79.
6 Ibid. 77-8.
7 Ibid. 83-4.
8 Ibid. 87, 64; *Letters on Yoga* 49, 50.
9 *Letters on Yoga* 192.
10 Ibid. 273, 54; *On Himself* 87, 116; Talk of 10 February 1940, published in Nirodbaran, *Talks*, ii & iii (combined edition 1985) 187.
11 *On Himself* 86.
12 Ibid. 49.
13 *Bande Mataram* 652, 659-60.
14 *On Himself* 86.
15 *The Synthesis of Yoga* 389.
16 *The Upanishads* 349-51. The translation from the Taittiriya Upanishad immediately above is from this commentary by Sri Aurobindo.
17 *On Himself* 68.
18 Ibid. 64.
19 *Karmayogin* 3.
20 *On Himself* 64; *Karmayogin* 4-5.
21 *On Himself* 64; cf. *The Synthesis of Yoga* 392.

CHAPTER 10
A SPIRITUAL ADVENTURE

1 *Letters on Yoga* 98.
2 *The Upanishads* 348.
3 *Letters on Yoga* 97 (two letters).
4 *On Himself* 109.
5 *The Supramental Manifestation* 291.
6 *The Synthesis of Yoga* 367-8.
7 Sri Aurobindo, *The Synthesis of*

Yoga 586; for more on Vedanta, Tantra and Sri Aurobindo's Yoga, see the pages that follow, Chapter 5 of the Introduction of the same book, and *Letters on Yoga* 39, 73.
8 *The Synthesis of Yoga* 586-7.
9 Ibid. 41-2.
10 Ibid. 389.
11 *On Himself* 64.
12 Undated letter, written shortly after 15 August 1912. Published (with incorrect date) *Supplement* 433.
13 Published in the semi-annual journal *Sri Aurobindo: Archives and Research* beginning with volume 10 (1986).
14 *On Himself* 469.
15 Ibid. 154.
16 *A&R* 11 (1987): 163.
17 Ibid. 171.
18 *The Synthesis of Yoga* 613; *Supplement* 508; *The Hour of God* 43.
19 *The Synthesis of Yoga* 613.
20 *Supplement* 375.
21 *On Himself* 426-7.
22 *The Synthesis of Yoga* 694.
23 *Supplement* 359ff; *The Synthesis of Yoga* 701ff.
24 *On Himself* 64.
25 *The Synthesis of Yoga* 429; *The Life Divine* 787-8.
26 *The Life Divine* 278.
27 *Letters on Yoga* 103.
28 *The Supramental Manifestation* 20-1.
29 *Letters on Yoga* 1234.

CHAPTER 11
A PHILOSOPHY OF EXPERIENCE

1 *On Himself* 374.
2 *Nirodbaran's Correspondence with Sri Aurobindo* 1066.
3 *On Himself* 84, 163.
4 *The Upanishads* 497.
5 *A&R* 7 (1983): 152.
6 *Essays on the Gita* 242.
7 Troy Organ, *Philosophy East &*

West 26 (1976): 353, 490–1.

8 *On Himself* 374; *A&R* 7 (1983): 165.

9 Troy Organ, *Philosophy East & West* 26 (1976): 491.

10 *The Life Divine* 19–20.

11 *On Himself* 383; *A&R* 7 (1983): 163–4.

12 *A&R* 7 (1983): 164.

13 Ibid. 165.

14 Ibid. 144.

15 Letter of 4 September 1934, published in *On Himself* 374.

16 *Letters on Yoga* 1281.

17 *A&R* 7 (1983): 165.

18 *The Life Divine* 2.

19 Ibid. 91, 714.

20 Ibid. 510, 835, 834.

21 Ibid. 1050, 1030, 1031, 1069, 1067.

22 *On Himself* 368–9.

23 *Social and Political Thought* 239.

CHAPTER 12
POET OF YOGA

1 *Collected Poems* 16.

2 Ibid. 46.

3 Ibid. 35.

4 Ibid. 51.

5 Ibid. 55–61.

6 Cousins 31, 30.

7 *On Himself* 276.

8 Letter of 22 June 1931, published in *The Future Poetry* 369–70.

9 *Collected Poems* 161.

10 Sri Aurobindo, letter of 4 January 1932 published in *The Future Poetry* 300; ibid. 17–18.

11 *Collected Poems* 563.

12 Ibid. 557.

13 *Collected Poems* 567.

14 *Collected Plays* 1.

15 *The Future Poetry* 74, 73.

16 *Collected Plays* 180.

17 *Collected Poems* 223.

18 Ibid. 248, 255, 257.

19 Ibid. 281.

20 *The Future Poetry* 6.

21 *Collected Poems* 391, 393.

22 *Savitri* 727–8.

23 Letter of 1946, published in *Savitri* 774.

24 *Savitri* 1–3.

25 Ibid. 671, 677.

CHAPTER 13
A LABORATORY EXPERIMENT

1 Letter of 1912, published (with incorrect date) in *Supplement* 433–4.

2 Ibid. 434.

3 *On Himself* 435.

4 *Supplement* 434.

5 Undated letter (April 1920), published in *A&R* 4 (1980): 17, 15 (translated from Bengali).

6 Letter to Dr Moonje 30 August 1920, published *On Himself* 432.

7 *On Himself* 479.

8 Letter of 26 March 1926, published in *Sri Aurobindo Circle* 32 (1976): 25, 26.

9 *A&R* 4 (1980): 21.

10 Talk of 4 May 1924: published in Purani, *Evening Talks* 443.

11 Talk of 18 May 1926, published in Purani, *Evening Talks* 326, 327, 328.

12 The Mother, *Collected Works* vii. 414 (translation emended).

13 *The Synthesis of Yoga* 376; see also 609, 627.

14 *Letters on Yoga* 157.

15 *Letters on Yoga* 1107–8.

16 *Supplement* 416.

17 *Letters on Yoga* 12.

18 The Mother, *Collected Works* vi. 297.

19 *On Himself* 375–6.

20 *Letters on Yoga* 139.

CHAPTER 14
LAST YEARS

1 Talk of 13 December 1938, published in Nirodbaran, *Talks* i. 24, 26, 27.

2 Maitra 103.
3 Report of speech at the East India Association, London, November 1943 (copy SAAA).
4 Letter Younghusband to D. K. Roy 17 December 1941, published in *Mother India* 27 (1975): 623.
5 See e.g. Dhirendra Mohan Datta, *The Chief Currents of Contemporary Philosophy* (Calcutta: University of Calcutta, 1961), and contributions by Kali Das Bhattacharya and others to *Sri Aurobindo: A Garland of Tributes*, a symposium edited by Arabinda Basu (Pondicherry: Sri Aurobindo Research Academy, 1973).
6 See Stephen H. Phillips, *Aurobindo's Philosophy of Brahman* (Leiden: E. J. Brill, 1986). Sri Aurobindo also has an important place in Robert Nozick's *Philosophical Explanations* (Cambridge: Harvard University Press, 1981), and will be dealt with in forthcoming books by Nozick and by Phillips.
7 Sri Aurobindo's principal champions are K. D. Sethna (*Sri Aurobindo — The Poet*, Pondicherry: Sri Aurobindo International Centre of Education, 1970); Sisirkumar Ghose (*The Poetry of Sri Aurobindo*, Calcutta: Chatuskone Private Limited, 1969), and K. R. Srinivasa Iyengar (*Indian Writing in English*, New Delhi: Sterling Publishers Private Limited, 1983); writers taking a dissenting view include P. Lal (*Modern Indian Poetry in English: An Anthology and a Credo*, 1969), Nissim Ezekiel (review cited in Sethna, op. cit.), and R.

Parthasarathy (Introduction to *Ten Twentieth-Century Indian Poets*, Delhi: Oxford University Press, 1987). For a more balanced and generally positive assessment see C. D. Narasimhaiah's *The Swan and the Eagle: Essays on Indian English Literature* (Shimla: Indian Institute of Advanced Study, 1987).
8 Review of *Poems* (1941) in *Modern Review* (undated cutting in SAAA).
9 Piper 132.
10 *On Himself* 399.
11 *On Himself* 404, 406.
12 Talk of 26 January 1940 (unpublished portion); cf. Purani, *Evening Talks* 734.
13 Munshi, 'Aurobindo Ashram — A Pilgrimage'; typewritten transcript of meeting (SAAA).
14 Letter Huxley to D. K. Roy 16 June 1948, published in *Mother India* 40 (1987): 467.
15 Nirodbaran, *Twelve Years* (1972): 264.

EPILOGUE

1 *Amrita Bazar Patrika* 8 December 1950.
2 *Hindusthan Standard*, 8 December 1950.
3 Ibid.
4 The Mother, *Collected Works of the Mother* xiii, 7.
5 Ibid.
6 Ibid. 199–200.
7 *On Himself* 138.
8 *On Himself* 151.
9 *The Life Divine* 883, 884.
10 *Social and Political Thought* 58; *The Life Divine* 1022.
11 *The Supramental Manifestation* 326.
12 *Letters on Yoga* 88.

Index